overexposure

A STORY ABOUT A SKIER

CHAD SAYERS

with Leslie Anthony and Taylor Godber

RMB
rmbooks.com

For information on purchasing bulk quantities of this book, or to obtain media excerpts or invite the author to speak at an event, please visit rmbooks.com and select the "Contact" tab.

RMB | Rocky Mountain Books Ltd.
rmbooks.com, @rmbooks, facebook.com/rmbooks

Cataloguing data available from Library and Archives Canada
ISBN 9781771605199 (hardcover)
ISBN 9781771605205 (electronic)

Project and Editorial Direction: Leslie Anthony
Cover and Page Design: Amélie Légaré, Calypso Design
Writing: Chad Sayers, Leslie Anthony and Taylor Godber
Slide Scanning and Colour Correction: Guy Fattal

Principal Photographers: Oskar Enander, Mattias Fredriksson, Jordan Manley, Paul Morrison, Steve Ogle, Daniel Ronnback, Chad Sayers, Jason Thompson
Additional Photographers: Eric Berger, David Carlier, Guy Fattal, Garrett Grove, Guillaume Le Guillou, Bruno Long, Kari Medig, Bruce Rowles, Ben Thouard, Don Weixl
Uncredited Photos: Chad Sayers
Front Cover Photos: Mattias Fredriksson (skiing); Jordan Manley (face)
Back Cover Photo: Jordan Manley

Printed and bound in China on FSC-certified paper.

We would like to also take this opportunity to acknowledge the traditional territories upon which we live and work. In Calgary, Alberta, we acknowledge the Niitsítapi (Blackfoot) and the people of the Treaty 7 region in southern Alberta, which includes the Siksika, the Piikuni, the Kainai, the Tsuut'ina and the Stoney Nakoda First Nations, including Chiniki, Bearpaw and Wesley First Nations. The City of Calgary is also home to Métis Nation of Alberta, Region III. In Victoria, British Columbia, we acknowledge the traditional territories of the Lkwungen (Esquimalt and Songhees), Malahat, Pacheedaht, Scia'new, T'Sou-ke, and W̱SÁNEĆ (Pauquachin, Tsartlip, Tsawout, Tseycum) peoples.

We acknowledge the financial support of the Government of Canada through the Canada Book Fund and the Canada Council for the Arts, and of the province of British Columbia through the British Columbia Arts Council and the Book Publishing Tax Credit.

Canada

Conseil des arts du Canada
Canada Council for the Arts

British Columbia
British Columbia Arts Council
An agency of the Province of British Columbia

Over the years, I've had the opportunity to work with many of the world's most talented ski photographers, each with a unique vision that has always expanded my own way of seeing things in the mountains.

Attuned to their canvas, the weather and the safety of their skiers, the monumental work ethic embraced by these alpine artists to capture the perfect shot can never be adequately honoured.

This book is dedicated to them.

Contents

Photo by Guy Fattal.

Foreword

BY JILL McDONALD

"After weeks of emotional anguish, I woke up one morning and decided to ski a La Grave classic with a few friends—a 2,150-metre couloir-studded run that included a technical rappel 1,400 metres downslope of the entrance... Taking the lead, I dropped in but skied haltingly, scared to let the surface snow run. Off-balance and riding the tails of my skis, physically drained from overthinking and not sleeping, nothing felt quite right. Yet this mission had been meant to heal all that ailed me."

Living the dream—any dream—is never what it appears. In action sports, cover shots come at a price, as does the lifestyle that supports them. For pro skiers the cost includes a steady diet of adrenaline, fear, ego, risk, injury, drive, emotion, loss and isolation. From the age of 18, Chad Sayers had lived that life in the frame of a camera, pursuing a perilous fall-line existence that led to this moment in the couloir. Now everything hung from a thin metal edge.

Overexposure.

Capturing images on snow bends the rules of photography. Reflected sunlight creates harsh shadows and blown-out highlights, so what a photographer sees through their lens is entirely different from what the camera registers. Where the eye sees a bright sunny day, the camera tracks dark, dirty and grey. To keep the snow white, a photographer lets in more light—the technique known as overexposure. On the other side of the camera, the skier lives their own version. The shooter tracks a hero shot, the machine probes its underbelly.

"The top section skied well, but as I descended towards a large rock that concealed the rappel anchor, I realized the couloir had frozen up. Soon it became too dangerous to ski, and I began to carefully sidestep towards the anchor, now 100 metres below... At each downward step I plugged a finger into the hard snow as a lifeline until, 10 metres from the rock, the snow met blue ice. A fall here meant a 600-metre death ride."

Chad Sayers is handsome and weathered, muscled and compact with an odd gait that cycles a story of injury and recovery. Internally wired and externally loose, no one really seems to know him, yet everyone has an emotional response when talking about him. Friends express both deep love and frustration; they may curse his habits but would join hands in a circle to shield him from the world. His identity, even to himself, is a Versailles Hall of Mirrors: skier, surfer, climber, traveller, photographer, spiritual pilgrim, shattered athlete, son, brother, father. The focal point of countless images capturing the purest form of gravity-driven motion, he is, and he is not, exactly what he appears.

Photography is a narrative tool. The frame controls what we see. Overexposure also seeks to be a narrative tool, provoking an emotional response. Playing to our assumptions, it can falsely validate what we perceive as real—the truth of an image. But the closer you look, the harder it is to discern detail; the photo quickly becomes pixelated, devolving into muddy patterns of light and dark. Pulling back, you're aware of something inherently uncomfortable in the process and know you're being fooled. The perfect turn isn't real. A stylish cliff jump doesn't prescribe a stylish landing, which can see broken bones, blown knees, shattered confidence.

At the height of his career, Sayers enjoyed sponsored trips to the world's most venerated ranges, expeditions, cover shots, film projects, support from brands. But living nowhere and everywhere, battling the chronic pain of injuries, it became a numbing circle of intensity that eroded his ability to feel and to share. He talked in circles around his own words, repeating emotions as if in a bid to feel them again, so deeply ingrained and reflected upon as to constitute their own form of numbness. Withdrawing, he found himself adrift between two poles: lured by the light but trapped in the dark.

"Gingerly, I stepped out on the ice. Sure enough, my ski slid out and I was left dangling by a finger... I had needed to experience the feeling that I wasn't in control of my life, my mind or the path ahead... And in that moment, I knew: I had to hang up my skis, get out of town and sort myself out."

Sayers the wide-eyed, freewheeling ski athlete became no one in particular. Bottled up and choking on the truth, he'd missed the transition to full responsibility. Masterfully manipulating reality was a living, but skiing passionately in pursuit of the next framed shot had also been destructive, breaking down the boundaries that others rely on to guide them through important life decisions. "Years ago, I crossed this line of solitude, and now I don't even know how to relate to the people I love," he wrote. His travel journals, often his only link to anything constant, brimmed with repetitions of loneliness and self-reflection, candour and confusion.

The road back was wide-ranging and rambling, an attempt to unravel the unravelling. To heal both physically and emotionally, Sayers explored the world, took a stance on the other side of the camera, tried to put himself in the shoes of people far less fortunate and far more wounded. Would it be enough to reclaim the light that set him on his journey?

Every photograph may be an interpretation, but together they still tell a story.

First time on skis at the family cottage in Ontario.

An Epiphany

SECTION I

MIGRATION

My childhood dream was to play in the National Hockey League like my idol, Wayne Gretzky. As with most small Ontario towns, Newcastle, where I spent my early years, was decidedly hockey-centric—we were on skates from the time we could walk. To help facilitate this goal, my dad watered down a homemade rink in the wee hours each night.

Chasing pucks with friends under a backyard spotlight and playing on a local hockey team moulded both my athleticism and mental game. I learned to stay on my feet and move quickly, to work as part of a team, to stay calm under pressure. Visualizing a play and then physically articulating what needed to happen to complete it came naturally. It was the same for all sports: given a singular focus and a milieu in which I could truly express myself, I excelled. That was good, because I was having serious trouble at school.

At age 10, I was diagnosed with severe attention-deficit disorder. I couldn't sit still or concentrate within a conventional education model. While hyper-awareness of everything unfolding around me was a superpower in sports, it was a handicap in the sensory-overload environment of a classroom. This diagnosis wasn't just challenging to myself, but also to those who had to deal with it, giving me a lifelong respect for the travails of schoolteachers.

Around that time, my family moved deeper into the Ontario hinterlands, with the plan of building a log home in the countryside. The area was beautiful. In summer, meadows filled with wildflowers and the grass turned gold; during winter, cold winds whipped across these same open spaces, building drifts and keeping rinks frozen. Best of all, there was plenty of room to dive into nature—running in the fields, riding dirt bikes between rows of corn, and just generally being outside all served to instill a sense of safety. I felt part of something bigger.

Eighteen months later, a nearly complete house stood proudly in the middle of our five-acre property while our temporary living quarters, a trailer, stood off to the side.

At the time, my father worked at General Motors in nearby Oshawa, where, flipping through a ski magazine on a break, a beautiful mountain landscape in British Columbia caught his eye. He allocated his next two-week holiday to checking out B.C. for new opportunities. Once there, driving around in a rental car, intuition directed him to what he was looking for. He called my mom from a pay phone and said, "Pack up—I found the place!"

13
CANADIEN

NESTING

Mom always trusted Dad's decisions, and though it was tough for my younger sister and I to leave friends, we were excited for a new adventure. Before we knew it, the house was finished and sold, and our belongings were shipped off in a moving truck. Along with two cats and a dog, we piled into a minivan to cross Canada and start a new life in Vernon, B.C.

I still remember the moment we entered the Rocky Mountains; I was wide-eyed and glued to the window, lost in the novelty of snow-clad peaks. Then came the aquamarine lakes and bright-green hills cradling the Okanagan Valley around Vernon, its vineyards and orchards washed by warm evening light against a dark blue sky. I was in total awe of our new surroundings, so different from where we'd lived before, with so much to explore.

I often wonder what would have happened if my parents hadn't taken that leap of faith. Who would I be? Would I have ever discovered mountains?

Early on, hockey was my life. Time spent on backyard rinks gave me a taste for what it was like to have a passion that required focus and determination. It has translated well to the mountains.

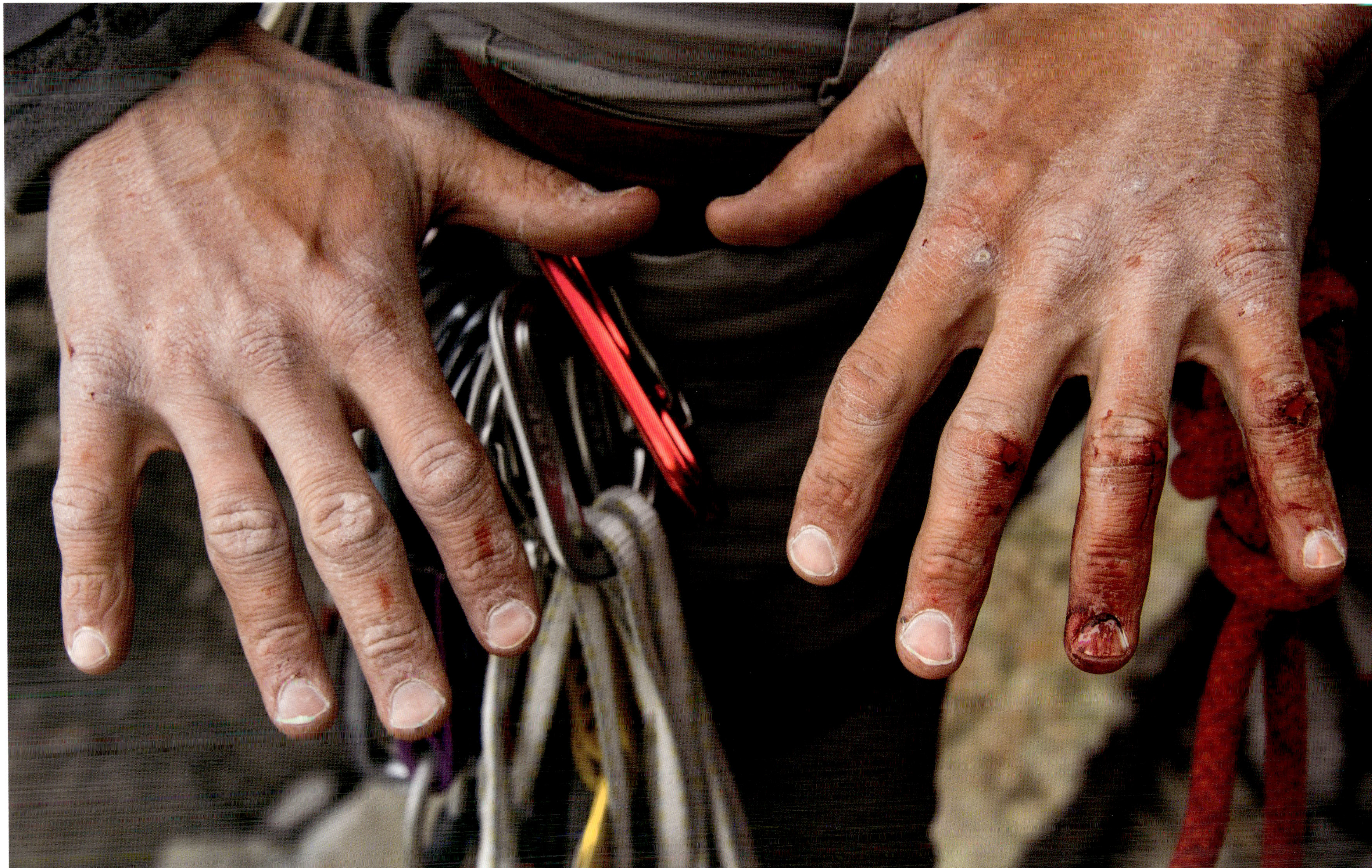

PREVIOUS SPREAD, RIGHT Exploring on Stewart Island, New Zealand. **ABOVE** Photo by Steve Ogle.

HATCHING

My earliest ski memory, from our first winter in Vernon, is of straight-lining a jump we'd built at the bottom of the driveway to launch over the road. Shortly afterward, a school program delivered my first real skiing experience at SilverStar Mountain, the ski area 10 minutes from our house. I was hooked.

I began spending evenings at the hill trying to keep up to kids who were better skiers, logging laps under the chair. In addition, plenty of solo time presented some of the sport's more aesthetic nuances: I remember staring into the night from the T-bar as snowflakes floated down to create perfect, powder-topped moguls. I loved the feeling of being on skis, of being in the mountains, of solitude.

My parents were a hundred percent behind my activities and poured everything they had into them. But they couldn't afford both skiing and hockey, so I was eventually presented with a classic Canadian conundrum: one or the other. It was an easy decision. I finished the hockey season that year and joined SilverStar's freestyle ski club.

Skiing moguls and launching big jumps set me on a path to what would soon be called professional freeskiing (as opposed to more rule-bound traditional disciplines of alpine racing and freestyle under the Fédération Internationale de Ski—or FIS). The club was a supportive environment, its coaches passionate about teaching kids the fundamentals. For some of us, weekend ski sessions soon progressed to serious training, travelling to regional competitions and pursuing the kinds of lines we'd seen in movies and magazines. A couple of club buddies and I started road-tripping every chance we got. Piling into a 1982 Ford pickup, we'd spark a joint, crank the Tragically Hip at full volume and chase our dreams in legendary B.C. ski resorts like Whitewater, Red Mountain and Whistler. In order to afford lift tickets, we slept in parking lots and ate a well-rounded diet of cheeseburgers and fries.

We drew inspiration from watching neck-deep Selkirk powder turns from our ski-film heroes like Trevor Petersen and Andrew Sheppard, or the mind-expanding performances of Shane McConkey and Seth Morrison. But the more ski culture we consumed, the more another decision loomed large: stay in Vernon, settle down and work a city job for the next 25 years, or move somewhere like Whistler and try to break into skiing's big leagues.

Photo by Jordan Manley.

A friend and I would often skip school and ski all the runs my mother wasn't patrolling as a ticket-checker. We got caught a few times, but Mom knew I had a future in skiing and supported it.

Early days with the freestyle club at SilverStar Mountain Resort, Vernon, B.C. Photos by Don Weixl.

ABOVE • RIGHT Climbing in the Bugaboos, Purcell Mountains, B.C. Photos by Steve Ogle.

FLEDGING

About the time I was finding my rhythm on the slopes, I was accepted into Earthquest, a Grade 11 outdoor education program more suited to my learning style—plenty of time spent outdoors and many hands-on projects. The four-month integrated curriculum included three separate week-long expeditions: backcountry skiing in the Monashees, ocean kayaking in Clayoquot Sound and backpacking in Cathedral Provincial Park.

Up to that point, I hadn't been exposed to true alpine or open-ocean environments, and the more I learned to navigate and understand the outdoors, the more I appreciated how vibrant and alive such environments truly were. I realized how important being connected to wilderness was and that I shouldn't waste time on things that didn't inspire me. The program also taught us about First Nations' philosophy and their approach to respecting the planet.

The following year, armed with a new suite of knowledge *and* a driver's licence, I split my free time between running and biking in Kalamalka Lake Provincial Park near Vernon, working on climbing skills in nearby Cougar Canyon, hiking in Glacier National Park, scrambling in the Alberta Rockies, fly fishing subalpine lakes in the Monashees—and learning how to use a camera to document it all. Collectively, these experiences helped me see a clear path; breaking away from my hometown to travel morphed from an option to a non-negotiable goal.

Problem-solving in Argentinian Patagonia. Photo by Steve Ogle.

Wild landscapes make me want to find the courage
to enter these unknown worlds and discover their secrets.

FLIGHT

On my first trip overseas in October of 1999, a friend and I strolled out of the Kathmandu airport into a cacophony of horns, idling vehicles and people screaming, shouting and hacking in the diesel-heavy air. From every direction drivers attempted to either charm or physically pull us into cabs. In the chaos we didn't know who to trust. Having forsaken the comforts and connections of home, I had been nervous about the unknowns of Nepal, but my desire to see an iconic landmark like Mt. Everest overpowered any fear.

After a stop in Kathmandu's infamous Thamel district—focal point for hippies, climbers, trekkers and all manner of Nepali street hustlers—we found ourselves jammed into the back of a truck with crates of chickens, overloaded backpacks and trekking permits to Everest base camp.

Choosing to hike unguided, we headed up a more indirect, less-congested route than the approach normally taken. The backdoor Gokyo Lakes circuit steered us down tight valleys, through tiny villages and over soaring ridges where we jostled with goats and yaks on steep, exposed trails. Each night we slept in humble family-run rest stops where, over a sunrise fire, we'd fuel up for the long day ahead on fresh chapati with jam and warm chai.

Though we had already taken several rest days above 3,000 metres to acclimatize, as we approached 5,000 metres the effects of altitude hit hard. Constant headaches and being out of breath even in the comfort of our sleeping bags was a new and strange sensation. On the final few days of our two-week approach, the first storm of the winter season rolled in, dusting us as we hiked and blocking any sight of the surrounding mountains. When the sky finally cleared, we found ourselves dumbfounded in the heart of the Himalaya: alpenglow illuminated an extraordinary view of the most beautiful peaks imaginable—Pumori, Nuptse, Lhotse and Everest. It was an epiphany, and at that point I knew what I wanted out of this short time on Earth.

Gokyo Lakes route to Everest base camp, Nepal.

LEFT Posing with ski-patrolling carabineros in Portillo, Chile. Photo by Jordan Manley. **RIGHT** Photo by Jordan Manley.

SOARING

After the Himalayan experience, I became absorbed in dreaming about mountains—where would my next adventure be?

A year later I stood in the empty streets of rustic Los Andes, Chile, frantically trying to flag down the area's lone cab. In English, I begged the driver to ferry me up the ladder of switchbacks that climbed to Portillo—a hotel-based ski resort set high in the mountains near the Argentine border—before an approaching storm closed the pass. Amazingly, he agreed.

A friend working as a ski instructor at Portillo had suggested I come down and experience the Andes. I took little convincing, and the excitement of skiing steep couloirs and climbing big lines at altitude quickly overrode the reality that I'd never travelled alone so far from home—nor did I speak any Spanish. My plan was to spend a month in Chile before exploring other parts of South America. As always, I counted on figuring it out as I went.

For the first time, I embraced the time-honoured role of a dirtbag ski bum—but without ski gear, which the airline had misplaced. I slept on the floor of the staff trailer and, with no means to order from the hotel dining room, poached the cafeteria line.

It took 10 days for my gear to arrive, and the sun came with it. The next few weeks were spent ski touring across frozen lakes, ascending chutes under the lift and skiing 1,500-vertical-metre road laps—everything I imagined the Andes to be and more.

I quickly felt at ease and full of energy in Chile, and knew it was the beginning of a new way of living—a life of travelling and embracing the unknown.

Portillo, Chile. Photos by Jordan Manley.

One day, Portillo's owner called me into her office. I thought for sure I'd be scolded for my unprofessional appearance and poaching tactics; instead, she offered me a free ski pass for the rest of the season and thanked me for my authenticity. She recognized my passion for skiing and that I wasn't in a state of financial fluidity like the pro skiers staying at the hotel.

Photo by Eric Berger

Whistler Days

SECTION II

WHISTLER

It was late fall and a dry start to the winter of 2000–2001 when I arrived in Whistler with everything I owned jammed into a truck. Though my sister lived there at the time, I knew no one else.

Perched in the window of a small cabin on a quiet afternoon as the season's first snowflakes made their way to the valley, I had an idea: I would cold-call Paul Morrison, a photographer whose work I admired, and ask if I could ski for him. My heart beat out of my chest as I reached for the phone book. Paul—a.k.a. the "King of Light"—was friendly on the line as I bravely planted the seed; he said he'd try to give me a ring later in the season.

Months later, on an April morning, I woke to that call. It had snowed 20 centimetres overnight and Paul asked if I could meet him at the bottom of Blackcomb Mountain in an hour. I scrambled out of bed, grabbed my gear and ran frantically for the bus.

On the ride into town I flashed back to my days working as a liftie at SilverStar. Cozied up in the T-bar hut during night shifts, I'd flip through skiing and climbing magazines, envisioning a move to the big mountains and seeing myself in those images. A Vernon photographer named Don Weixl had provided my first opportunities to ski in front of a lens, teaching me how to nail the mark by being in the most dynamic body position when he pressed the shutter. After seeing photos that confirmed I got it right, the adrenaline surge of ski modelling had me hooked.

On Blackcomb, Paul and I scoped out a nice seven-metre cliff. I cleaned the take-off, took one last look at the landing below, and stepped back up the hill to get the proper speed—it was the moment of truth I'd moved to Whistler for.

When a frame from that session became the cover of the February 2002 issue of revered *Powder* magazine, I was acutely aware that my dream was becoming reality.

LEFT Sunrise in the Tantalus Range, Squamish, B.C. Photo by Jordan Manley. **ABOVE** Photo by Paul Morrison.

Photos by Paul Morrison.

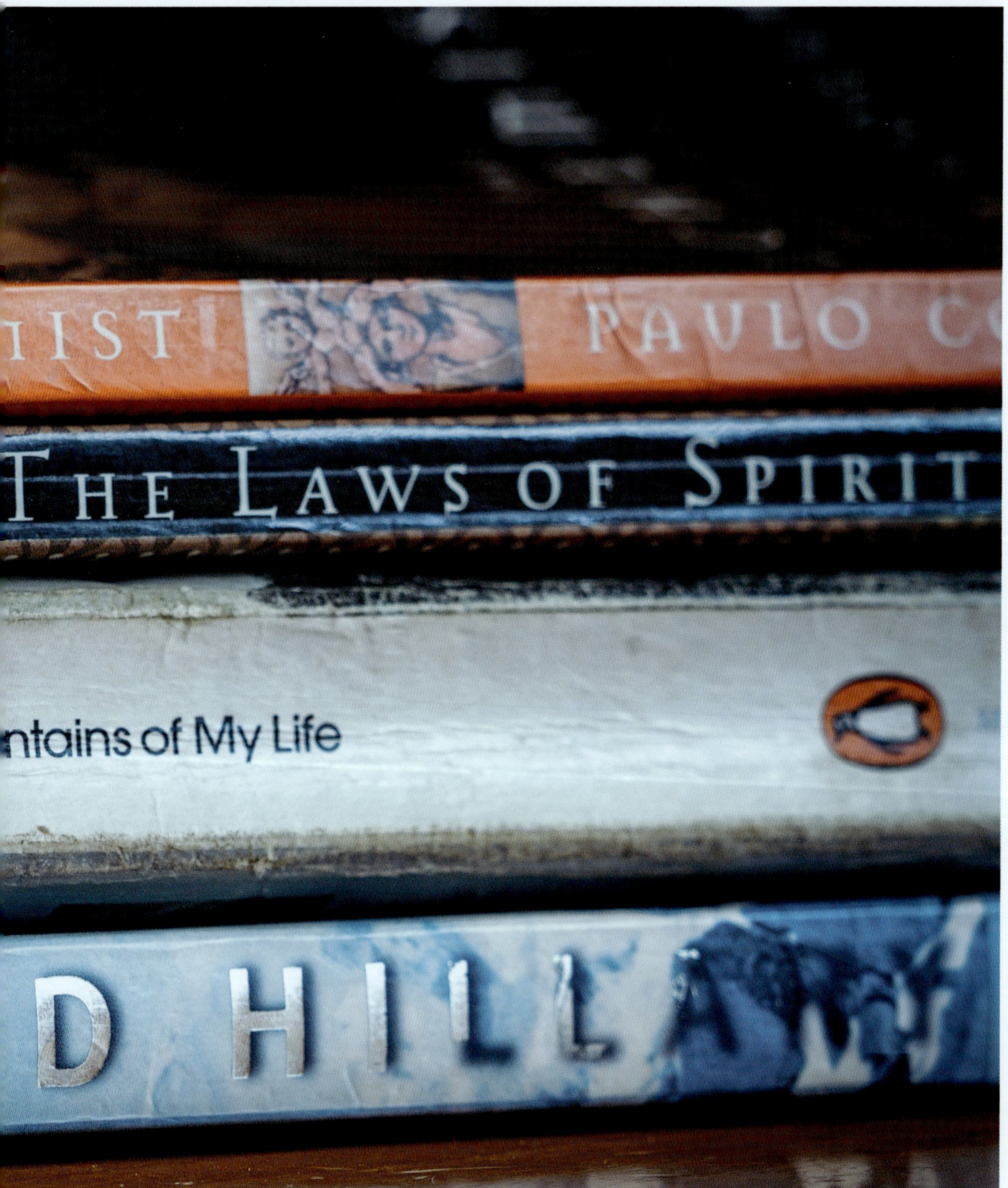
PAULO
THE LAWS OF SPIRIT
of My Life
HILL

FOCUS

I was nobody when I started skiing professionally, just another young guy who wanted to be in magazines and movies. But I felt confident and inspired, feeding off the high energy and world-class talent in Whistler at the time—a genuine vanguard of both progressive freestyle and the "big-mountain" movement of off-piste freeskiing. Park and pipe pioneers Mike Douglas and the New Canadian Air Force were my inspiration, as well as skiers like PY LeBlanc and Hugo Harrisson, Whistler-based French Canadians leading the freeskiing world tour and pushing up-and-comers like myself to perform. Still, I was plagued by questions. What was I trying to accomplish? What would take me to the next level?

An old joke starts with the question *How do you get to Carnegie Hall?* The answer is practice, practice, practice. The same goes for skiing. Becoming a great skier is mostly about mileage. In Whistler, I started skiing harder, pushing my limits, lapping Blackcomb Mountain top to bottom, day in and day out, charging off anything I could find. Mostly I skied alone to avoid distractions or being held back; having only terrain to overcome brought a deeper connection with the mountains and with my physical self-expression—a true exploration of skiing as art.

Skiing the resort was free of pressure, but there would be more serious energy to navigate when I made the move to the competition scene. With 50 or more skiers ready to throw down and win at any contest, fear, ego, defeat and victory always mingled in the air. And yet for a while I felt indestructible. I wasn't a big-time star, but I was skiing my best and felt in sync and powerful. I was still too naïve to know that such confidence, so necessary to perform, could also kill me.

LEFT Photo by Jordan Manley. **RIGHT** In deep at Shames Mountain ski area, Terrace, B.C. Photo by Jordan Manley.

LEFT Photo by Mattias Fredriksson. **RIGHT** Photo by Jordan Manley.

Coast Mountains, Bella Coola, B.C. Photo by Mattias Fredriksson.

Though I love being out in the mountains with friends, there's something special
about fuelling a dream solely from self—finding determination from a calling
that speaks to you from the inside when you're skiing alone.

Photo by Jordan Manley.

INDUSTRY

Shortly after the *Powder* cover shot, I received my first cheque and a bunch of gear from a ski sponsor—it wasn't much, but it felt like a lottery win.

Back in the day, ski athletes had to hustle to get support. As was quickly becoming my habit, I'd cold-called a ski brand, introduced myself, and told them why I wanted to ski for them. Landing a spot in a movie would require similar chutzpah. Prior to social media, taking initiative to establish yourself in the industry was the only path.

With a respected brand behind my name, there was now more incentive for shooters to sell images of me, and everything started to flow. Editorial and film trips ensued; I attended international competitions and planned expeditions to places I'd only dreamed of, making my way into the worlds of ski culture and ski business together. As the opportunities grew, so did the cheques, and I was eventually able to put an end to random summer work like construction and painting.

Understanding the ebb and flow of the ski industry was key, but so was the art of authenticity, investing time in building relationships and standing up for myself. Real partnerships took perseverance, and the test of their stability came when multiple injuries began to plague me. Some connections were lost immediately—there was always a healthier up-and-comer in line. Other unions strengthened; like family, these companies understood the lifestyle, the risks taken, the passion behind a skier's commitment. In those times, a sense of mutual trust and respect really stood out.

Knowing the right people was important, but at the end of the day it always came down to what you were willing to put on the line to stay relevant. Basically, you still had to perform.

I always dreamed of being in ski movies and worked hard to make it happen. I've made hundreds of phone calls and once drove 24 hours solo to knock on the door of a film company.

LEFT • RIGHT Coast Mountains, Bella Coola, B.C. Photos by Mattias Fredriksson.

Khyber Pass, Whistler Mountain, Whistler, B.C. Photo by Jordan Manley.

ROOTS

The taste of orchard-fresh fruit and the sensation of running through swaying grasses had imprinted upon me growing up in Vernon, but I've since found similar essences that speak *home* to me in every corner of the world: the heat of El Salvador, the culture of Patagonia, the vibe of Hawaii. The list is lengthy: Costa Rica, Indonesia and La Grave are other places that instantly register a sense of belonging, safety, familiarity, love. One place, however, stands out for the smell of fresh air and the sight of snow-clad mountains in the distance—Whistler.

I lived in several places in Whistler over my many years there, but the decade spent at a friend's place nestled along Fitzsimmons Creek, a minute's walk from Blackcomb Mountain, was formative. I could come and go at will, be away weeks or even months, and return to the comfort of a world unchanged—my pictures on the walls, Persian rug on the floor, sentimental objects on familiar perches. When goodbyes became the norm, my last act was always a visual scan of that room, unsure if I would make it back.

The travelling life of sleeping in different beds, eating random foods and being perpetually exhausted was changing me. The more I travelled, the more I appreciated the creature comforts of Whistler—falling asleep to the sound of the raging creek, going for a run on my favourite forest trail, drinking tea on the porch at sunset.

Coming home to Whistler became a way to put everything experienced on a journey or over a season into perspective. Ultimately, however, even that would need to change. On a chairlift ride in Switzerland with my friend, I learned that he and his partner were expecting a baby and would need more space.

A perk of living in Whistler was the amount of easily accessed backcountry—what skiers call slackcountry. There was so much untouched big-mountain terrain just a short hike from the lifts that it could feel like a separate resort. I quickly learned that these areas were the training grounds for many of Canada's most prolific freeskiers. During my first few years there, on big powder days I'd race to the lifts frothing over the chance to be first up Spanky's Ladder and into Ruby Bowl, or to bag a steep line down DOA—the classic couloir off Blackcomb Peak.

Photos by Jordan Manley.

LEFT Whistler Mountain, Whistler, B.C. Photo by Jordan Manley. **RIGHT** Photo by Jordan Manley.

COMPETITION

The year I moved to Whistler I also qualified for the Freeride World Tour, and competition became my life.

Driven to succeed, the idea of winning the tour consumed me. Not because I *needed* to be the best, but because I felt deep inside that I had what it took—the stamina and strength to make it safely to the bottom in one high-speed shot. I'd also acquired the right mindset: I could now control the surge of adrenaline in the start gate while visualizing the run, knowing just how fast and at which angles to send it off mountain features without hesitating.

Seven years in the competition game brought many proud highlights: first place at an event in Switzerland, and second place two years running in the Canadian Freeskiing Championships. Along with the wins, however, came numerous wrecks, one of which ended up on a television sports channel's "Top 100 Crashes" highlight reel. That tumble had taken place as my father watched in terror, certain I would die as I rag-dolled down the mountain. Nevertheless, he continued to encourage me. I was so determined in those years that I never questioned for a second what I was doing—so no one else did either.

2003 Canadian Freeskiing Championships, Blackcomb Mountain, Whistler, B.C. Photo by Bruce Rowles.

PREMONITION

White-knuckled behind the wheel of my truck, I was heading to Snowbird, Utah, for the 2006 U.S. Freeskiing National Championships. In my prime and really going for it, everyone on the tour knew how badly I wanted the title and that I just might be ready for it. But when I pulled over on an open stretch of Nevada highway to relieve myself, an unwelcome feeling infiltrated my haze of confidence: an intuitive sense that I was due for a crash. I'd been pushing the envelope, fearlessly going faster, taking more risks and getting away with it. Now I saw myself either dying or having a serious fall. I got back in the truck and shook off the apparition, refocusing for the contest to come.

At Snowbird I met up with a few buddies for some pre-contest training. Conditions were epic—a clear afternoon with 40 centimetres of cold, light snow. I lined up a 12-metre cliff right at the bottom of the venue and took my time getting into the takeoff, nailing it cleanly and stomping the landing. *I'm ready for this* I thought to myself. Just one more lap.

I went back up to session the same cliff. Skiing into the line full power, I made four solid turns in sloughing snow that cascaded around the steep, rocky in-run and through a bottleneck choke. Unlike my previous run, however, at the last second I clipped a hidden rock and was sent flying headfirst towards a large boulder. I took the impact on the left side of my body and continued to flip through the air off the cliff before landing in a heap among some trees. I found my left leg up around my head and, after throwing it back downslope and coughing blood into the snow, realized I had snapped my femur and suffered some internal injuries.

I remained conscious right up until the moment they put me under for surgery. The rescue crew helicoptered me to a hospital where it was determined that in addition to a broken femur, I had a smashed pelvis, broken ribs and a punctured lung. I spent a post-surgery week recovering, but when I was taken off intravenous drugs and released, I foolishly thought *Yeah, I'm good—I don't need any more pain meds.* A friend picked me up from the hospital in my truck and dropped me back at the hotel before leaving to attend the weeklong event's final party.

Waking up in the middle of the night, I finally realized how significant my injuries were. Now in excruciating pain, I dragged myself to the bathroom and flipped on the light: staring back from the mirror was a body black and blue from head to toe. Aware of how much damage I had done and what was ahead, I broke down and cried.

LEFT Photo by Mattias Fredriksson. **RIGHT** Kicking Horse Mountain Resort, Golden, B.C. Photo by Mattias Fredriksson.

On the freeskiing tour, many venues are "visual inspection only," meaning you can't ski them before the competition. So you have no idea where rocks are, how the snow might feel, or how much speed is needed to hit a cliff and make the landing. All of this has to be studied and determined from afar—but I'm becoming good at it.

LEFT Photo by Jordan Manley. **RIGHT** Photo by Mattias Fredriksson.

RECONCILIATION

Two years later I returned to the Snowbird competition and stood atop the same run, intent on skiing it again. The accident here, as well as a subsequent blown knee, had shown me that I wasn't indestructible; but though I now had to cope daily with deep leg pain, it hadn't frightened me enough to quit this type of skiing. *That* was the scary part.

One thing that had shifted was my state of mind. The ability to look at the mountain from afar, envision myself skiing and feel the sensations of every turn—the out-of-body experience, if you will—had diminished.

Still, I skied solidly that day without a moment of uncertainty. It would be the last time I ever competed, the end of an era but the beginning of a new outlook and a burning desire to dig deeper, charge harder and want whatever it was I was chasing even more.

Photo by Mattias Fredriksson.

The Alps

SECTION III

ARRIVAL

I spent my first night at a European ski resort in what would become a recurring tableau: curled up for the night on my ski bag in front of the Chamonix train station. My fervour to see the lustrous peaks of the Mont Blanc massif—scene of many of the heroic tales of alpine death and glory I'd consumed as a young skier—made the frigid arrangement acceptable. En route to Les Arcs for the 2001 European Freeride World Tour Championships, I'd felt that a stopover in Chamonix was *de rigueur*; I needed to take in the energy of such a holy place for skiers.

On the bus from the train station to the famed Aiguille du Midi, through the organized mayhem that swept me from the ticket counter onto the 60-person tram, it was clear everyone was here to participate in a revered and historic ski culture. A mixed bag of characters was drawn to Chamonix: hardcore French guides with faces like weathered stone, well-outfitted Swedish ski bums, the idle rich and famous popping champagne at the top. Morning parking lots were a scatter of beautiful mountain girls coiling rope and racking climbing harnesses with ice screws while dirtbag skiers washed dishes from the night before next to their filthy vans. The après-ski scene was an equal mishmash of locals, tourists, big-name film crews and ski pros celebrating another day of glory—and survival—in the mountains.

My first ski day, alone on the bridge that spans the gap between two pinnacles on the Aiguille du Midi summit, I admired the raw beauty of rock, ice and fresh snow surrounding me. A cold wind and bright sun washed my face with a single question: did I have what it took to climb these massive faces, ski these fabled steeps, live life on such an edge?

Boarding Switzerland's famous Glacier Express train.
Photo by Mattias Fredriksson.

LEFT Stopping for lunch at a pizzeria in La Thuile, Italy. Photo by Mattias Fredriksson. **RIGHT** Photo by Mattias Fredriksson.

After a big, cold storm in Chamonix, I was hustling for a ski partner at the Aiguille du Midi tram when local Oli Herren and ski legends Glen Plake and Bruno Compagnet said I could tag along. Stepping out at the top, heart pumping, I followed their tracks towards the Cosmiques Couloir—a steep, sought-after classic. As we skied into the entrance to assess conditions, I heard only a few words in French exchanged. Without hesitating or removing their skis, my companions began downclimbing the first 60 metres—which usually requires a rappel. I had to follow suit, stepping carefully down the steep face, where no mistake could be made. When my edges finally left rock and ice, I skied out into the 50-degree chute as the others disappeared into the void like snow ghosts. I chased them down 800 metres of light, deep powder to the glacial seracs at the bottom, grateful to ski a Chamonix classic in classic conditions.

LEFT A couloir off of the Brévant Flégère ski area in Chamonix, France. Photo by Daniel Ronnback. **RIGHT** Photo by Daniel Ronnback.

I'm back at it, skiing around the Alps for a few months, living out of my pack, working with the best ski photographers in the world. But I'm noticing a numbness and confusion around transitioning from a life in the mountains to living in what society deems a normal reality.

I'm constantly unsure where I belong in the world.

LEFT Photo by Oskar Enander. **RIGHT** Navigating a larch forest on the Monte Rosa in Gressoney, Italy. Photo by Jordan Manley.

ALPS

For many skiers, the Alps symbolize the very essence of freedom—an arena of endless possibility that draws one back again and again. The moment I stepped out of the Aiguille du Midi tram on that first trip, a whole new world opened to me. I had no ski partner, no idea where to go and was still learning how to manage powder on steep slopes. Open crevasses, unmarked slopes, exposed ice—*What did I want from all this?*

At first it was overwhelming to be amongst such big mountains. The Alps stretch 1,200 kilometres across eight countries and are geologically diverse, from the granite spires of Chamonix to the limestone castles of Italy's Dolomites. Despite these differences, there's a similarity to how skiing is celebrated across the range—more a way of life than the recreational cult it's treated as in North America—and I knew it was something I wanted to be part of. Among the many things learned here were how to scope competition lines, why and how to listen to the mountains at all times, paying close attention to those more experienced than yourself, and the importance of choosing ski partners you can trust. Key nuances of ski culture were also instilled—like how to inhale an espresso and *pain au chocolat* at the bottom of a tram line, or jump trains with heavy ski bags.

After dozens of trips over the years, time spent in the Alps offered a welcome cocktail of anarchy and connection that often helped me recognize my own shadow in the snow. Moments spent teetering on steep slopes over serious exposure demanded I get out of my head, while nights spent walking streets alone, introspecting on church steps, watching smoke from hand-rolled cigarettes dance in the cold air of cafés, combined to create a spiritual port of call.

Staring up from deep valleys into a swirl of clouds and peaks, I was overcome by a longing to push my limits in ever-more-demanding environments and by the thought that *this* was the hold the Alps had on its inhabitants. Nothing else mattered when I clicked into my skis; the dream held so long in my mind's eye always felt attainable here.

My recollections of the Alps are rich with descents that made my heart sing, like the day Andreas Fransson, photographer Mattias Fredriksson and I skied the enormous Marbrées Couloir on the Italian side of Mont Blanc in 50 centimetres of fresh snow during a whiteout. Worried the entire time that the slope would rip out and kill us, we eventually broke through clouds into the larch forests of Courmayeur's Val Ferret and the tension evaporated. Alpenglow lit the sky as we embraced and celebrated the beauty of the moment.

Photo by Mattias Fredriksson.

Photos by Oskar Enander.

Skiing is about being completely alive and free in the moment, in your
heart, in each breath, in every turn. It has become my soul—a gift,
a truth, an expression, a passion, a job and so much more.

LEFT Photo by Mattias Fredriksson. **RIGHT** Brévant Flégère ski area, Chamonix, France. Photo by Mattias Fredriksson.

ANDREAS

I had been an admirer of Andreas Fransson—a Swedish freeskier known for his humble demeanour and passion for skiing the steepest of steeps—for many years. When I finally had the honour of meeting him, it included a plan to ski together for two weeks in his adopted home of Chamonix. I also hoped to sponge up any wisdom shared from his famously wild mind.

The first line we skied foreshadowed how much Andreas would humble me during our time together. The aim that day was to ski a steep, exposed couloir that led to a rappel, then onto a massive, dog-legging face above serious exposure. We moved efficiently through the couloir, laying precise turns down a strip of snow between granite walls. The depth of our conversations—about love and philosophy and what it meant to be free-spirited—calmed my nerves through the intensity of the descent.

Having longed to crew up with someone who'd help me push my own steep skiing, and feeling confident in his presence, I accepted Andreas's invitation to lead a section. Traversing into the middle of the face and turning downward, snow sloughed around me as I fought to stay on my now-frozen feet. Crossing some crusty spines in search of the line, however, I was thrown off my footing. In an instant, I realized my worst nightmare, tumbling violently backwards down the 50-degree slope. Knowing it could be the end, I clawed desperately at the snow to slow my descent. Then, miraculously, everything stopped spinning. I was sprawled spread-eagle, chest to the mountain, just above the point of no return. It wasn't my first or last brush with death, but it was definitely my closest.

Despite the severity of the situation, I gathered myself together and finished the line. Andreas hadn't seen what happened and when he eventually joined me I kept the entire thing to myself. For whatever reason, I didn't feel the need to share; it may have been ego, but I'd also come to a place where close calls no longer rattled me. The logic might seem twisted, but it was more an acknowledgement of the risks we were taking and how quickly things could slip away.

It was natural for Andreas to lead visiting skiers around Chamonix, and so it had been a rookie mistake for me to accept the role of lead. I gratefully followed his rhythm the remainder of our time together, our ski styles and communication a good fit.

A couple years later I was devastated to hear that Andreas had died in an avalanche in Chile, another friend and inspiration lost to the mountains we both loved.

Andreas Fransson in his happy
place, Chamonix, France.
Photo by Mattias Fredriksson

LEFT Engelberg, Switzerland. Photo by Oskar Enander. **RIGHT** Photo by Daniel Ronnback.

LEFT Photo by Mattias Fredriksson. **RIGHT** Three hours of waiting for a 30-second window of light. Engelberg, Switzerland. Photo by Oskar Enander.

The taste of true solitude—where there's enough mental space to hear the internal conflicts—either draws people in or scares them away.

LEFT Argentière Basin, Chamonix, France. Photo by Daniel Ronnback. **RIGHT** Photo by Daniel Ronnback.

LEFT • RIGHT Photos by Daniel Ronnback.

Now I see why climbing mountains is a way of life. Chasing these incredible moments on rock, ice and snow—so pure, so beautiful, so unexpected and enlightening—really speaks to my core.

LEFT Couloir Cosmique, Aiguille du Midi, Chamonix, France. Photo by Daniel Ronnback. **RIGHT** Photo by Daniel Ronnback.

As alpine transitions to valley, skiers inevitably find themselves in the trees and often stop to admire these sacred storm sanctuaries. At home in British Columbia, the forests are ancient and huge, the evergreen boughs of tall spruce and fir finely evolved to hold snow and shed it to their roots. In the Alps, however, forests are dominated by non-evergreen larch that shed their needles each fall to stand naked through the winter. Still, they have their own uniqueness and glow, and it only took a few trips before skiing them felt safe and familiar—a home away from home.

AFTERLIFE

Adrenaline coursed through my veins as I peered into the mist below. Despite the inevitability of its appearance in such situations, I was annoyed that the infernal question of justification had arisen again—*Was I meant to keep pushing it like this?* Still, I preferred it posed as a question than some of the more imaginative broadcasts of my mind, which often included visions of falling, followed by the disturbingly vivid brutality of impact.

Above the mist, Alpine choughs soared in clear skies, playful birds believed to be winged symbols of the restive spirits of fallen climbers and skiers. I now counted several friends among them and couldn't help contemplate the validity of this lifestyle—of conscious immersion in risky terrain that yielded serious consequences when things didn't go as planned.

But like the soaring choughs, I always circled back: what looked like a death wish to others felt like no more than a devotion to discovery for me—not to mention a job. I reminded myself that in order to stay on my feet and out of the spiralling column of lost souls, I needed to simply accept that chasing something so pure, yet so dangerous, was the life I had chosen.

LEFT Photo by Jordan Manley. **RIGHT** Courmayeur Mont Blanc, Italy. Photo by Mattias Fredriksson.

LEFT Exiting the Punta Helbronner tram, Courmayeur Mont Blanc, Italy. Photo by Mattias Fredriksson. **RIGHT** Photo by Mattias Fredriksson.

Photo by Mattias Fredriksson.

A Skier's Journey

SECTION IV

Interior of a high-altitude hut in the Zagros Mountains, Iran. Photo by Jordan Manley.

LAUNCH

The relationship between skier and photographer can be an intimate one. Working in a harsh environment, often far from home, pushing into an unpredictable alpine labyrinth of light and shadow requires the kind of trust and mutual respect that can forge deep friendships. Such was the case with photographer Jordan Manley.

In 2009 he and another longtime ski partner, Forrest Coots, floated a concept for a unique series of short ski films that would document our own particular path in the ski world. *A Skier's Journey* was born.

We all shared the common threads of curiosity and a desire to break from the current ski industry formula of big-production films depicting who could send it off the biggest cliff and ski the toughest line—a high-stakes derivative of the contest world I'd just transitioned out of. Instead, we hoped to capture something more genuine and heartfelt—the kind of soulful expression shared through a collective drive to travel, to be in the mountains, to understand new cultures. It would also offer a different pace of life.

The new focus brought more purpose and style to my skiing—a way to give back for all the light and beauty I'd been blessed with in the mountains, which I hoped could inspire viewers to overcome their fears and live their own dreams.

Over the course of seven years we travelled widely, investing our every ounce of energy, courage and money in the endeavour. We exposed ourselves to endless hazards, both natural and human, as well as powerful and sacred landscapes. We were a vagabond family, dragging gear from one airport to the next, feverishly focused on the next remote ski destination. We shed blood, sweat and tears, but there were also plenty of smiles.

At times the process pushed us to the brink. While some moments brought out my best—where I skied from the heart and felt passionate about travel, mountains and skiing—other moments delivered the shadow side of physical hardship, personality clashes, painful shifts in perspective, awareness of insecurities and paralyzing uncertainty.

One key realization was that the series very much reflected what I had been doing on my own through expeditions to remote locales, a life I would continue leading once the cameras stopped rolling. In the end, skiing where no one else had ever done so—with its deeper meaning of discovery, leaving tracks that would only be swept away by the wind—made it all worthwhile.

The Skier's Journey crew had one of its strangest snow experiences on the edge of one of the largest sand deserts on the planet. Inside a luxury shopping mall in Dubai, capital of the United Arab Emirates, we found a dedicated international ski community—lapping slopes of artificial snow in a refrigerated "ski area"—as addicted as we were to the sensation of gliding on snow.

LEFT • RIGHT Dubai, United Arab Emirates. Photos by Jordan Manley.

LEFT Visiting a traditional *onsen* in Hokkaido, Japan. Photo by Jordan Manley. **RIGHT** Photo by Jordan Manley.

I try to remain humble yet faithful to both the brightest and darkest parts of my life. I believe that intuition is the greatest gift we are given, and trusting its vibrations an act of divine faith.

LEFT • RIGHT Westfjords, Iceland. Photos by Jordan Manley.

LEFT • RIGHT Ski touring in the midnight sun, Stjernøya, Norway. Photos by Mattias Fredriksson.

A springtime assignment for Powder *magazine found me north of the Arctic Circle in Norway, ski-touring on Stjernøya Island with a stellar crew. Cold ocean lay still and dark as we admired the view from the bow of a 25-metre wooden sailboat after a dinner of reindeer stew. A lone whale breached in a fjord hung with silken waterfalls. Taking a Zodiac to the far side, we scrambled up a steep ridge, intent on an evening ski despite the midnight sun sitting too low to brighten the slopes. Stopping to admire the area's wild beauty, I saw a rabbit's foot lying atop vibrant green moss. An omen? At the top, gazing at the sailboat anchored below, we prepared for a shadowy 600-metre descent. Just then, golden rays broke through the peaks to wash the perfectly softened snow in gold and copper. The rabbit's foot delivered.*

LEFT Photo by Jordan Manley. **RIGHT** Shemshak ski area in the Alborz Mountains, Iran. Photo by Jordan Manley.

KASHMIR

Episode One of *A Skier's Journey* documented a trip to Gulmarg in the isolated Kashmir region of northern India, which was embroiled in a longstanding conflict with Pakistan. We exited the airport in Srinagar into a war zone—surrounded by bunkers laced with barbed wire and manned by armed young men ready for action. It was a harsh introduction.

Loading into a jeep, we began making our way to the mountains. Ten minutes later we were stopped by masked men throwing rocks, and I saw the fear in our driver's eyes as he skirted them. Politics was one of many obstacles faced here; another was a serious snow drought. The latter, at least, was solved when a long-awaited storm finally rolled through, dropping several metres of snow. Unfortunately, the avalanche danger also became extreme. Aiming for lower terrain, we skied long, deep-powder runs through empty forests, spilling into villages where we'd catch a ride back to Gulmarg under sunset skies.

Meanwhile, I had a serious issue: the leg pain I'd been suffering for years by this point had consumed me. I did my best to ski on the good leg, lingering over 4,000-metre-high views from the top of the world's loftiest gondola, surrounded by bored, heavily armed soldiers smoking hash. But one morning, as I awoke to monkeys howling outside my window, the pain in my leg had become so searing that I knew I couldn't ski. I had to find some real medicine—not the ineffective ibuprofen I was eating like candy or locally available analgesic creams. Pakistan and its lax over-the-counter drug laws were 20 minutes away, so I paid a guy to drive me there. On the way I laid out my plan: I'd stay in the jeep and he'd give some money to the border guards, explain what I needed, then return with the goods. I looked him in the eyes and said: "I need *pain pills*—not cream!"

After 45 minutes of nervous waiting, the driver returned with a paper bag. Reaching into it with high hopes of medicinal salvation, I pulled out yet another tube of cream. The next six weeks on the road were rough ones.

Photo by Jordan Manley.

You can lose friends, lose faith or lose your mind and then find them all again. But every landscape of self is destroyed when the body is consumed by pain. Often, you're unsure if you will survive it.

LEFT The 3,750-metre gondola top station at Gulmarg ski area in Kashmir, India. Photo by Jordan Manley. **RIGHT** Photo by Daniel Ronnback.

Bucharest, Romania. Photo by Jordan Manley.

ROMANIA

I arrived in Romania solo, during a 50-year storm cycle that was hitting the country hard. Stepping into a cold, clear night, I hailed a cab to the centre of Bucharest.

Cracks and scars on abandoned buildings spoke to the violent civil unrest of the Romanian Revolution decades earlier. On the street, people's eyes reflected both survival and the challenge of a brand new set of troublesome conditions, as they worked to keep their fires lit and homes from collapsing under the relentless snow.

At my hotel, I embraced the unique but familiar feeling of being outside the walls of my own comfortable existence and submerged in a different way of life. In the morning, blurry with jet lag, I pulled back the blinds to the despairing sight of rain. I tried to let go of any expectations for the month ahead.

When the rest of the crew arrived, we lugged our ski and film gear through busy streets to a dark and dingy train station. We laughed at how out of place we looked, drawing repeated glares from dodgy characters as we struggled to get our oh-so-foreign-looking gear onto the train before the whistle blew. A 15-hour night ride would hopefully deliver us to colder, snowier environs. Thick cigarette smoke leaked through the walls from the adjacent cabin as we dozed between our piles of baggage.

Days passed, then weeks, and the food, people and ever-present history of the former Eastern Bloc made for great footage and cultural experiences, but ski conditions continued to deteriorate. Many times over the years I'd stared out a window watching rain fall in the middle of winter, longing for a return of colder temperatures and better conditions—a wait we called "the slow roast." But after a final seven days bunked up in a hotel room with a crew of equally frustrated guys, it seemed more of a crying shame.

A life of travel teaches that you get what you get on expeditions, and it's up to you to make the most of it. Though we could all look each other in the eye and say we tried, unable to suffer the slow roast any longer, we bailed.

LEFT Monastery of Saint Ivan of Rila, Rila Mountains, Bulgaria. Photos by Jordan Manley. **RIGHT** Sunrise climb on Mt. Erclyes, Turkey. Photo by Daniel Ronnback.

I feel that it's my obligation at this
moment in life to stay on my feet and
fulfill the dreams I have as a skier
before I head down a different road.

LEFT Photo by Jordan Manley. **RIGHT** Ben Nevis, Scotland. Photo by Bruno Long.

LEFT Westfjords, Iceland. Photo by Jordan Manley. **RIGHT** Photo by Jordan Manley.

You invest so much time and energy into planning expeditions, getting sponsors and traveling to remote ski destinations, then often have an experience far from what you'd hoped for. The lesson is to have no expectations and ask nothing more from the mountains than a bit of wisdom, safe passage and fresh perspective.

Stuck in Europe with the Alps dry and no snow in the forecast, we were scanning weather maps when we noticed a big storm about to hit central Turkey. Changing plans, we spent the next few weeks touring the slopes of Mount Erciyes, an enormous volcano dominating the Cappadocia skyline. We skied some of the deepest, driest powder imaginable until we were ready to drop, a perfect reason to visit an 800-year-old hammam, or Turkish bath, one of the country's oldest traditions.

LEFT The Mt. Erciyes volcano looms over the city of Kayseri, Turkey. Photo by Daniel Ronnback. **RIGHT** Photo by Daniel Ronnback.

Photo by Jordan Manley.

BAFFIN

I underestimated the hostility of the weather on Baffin Island in the Canadian High Arctic, a remote landscape where indescribable cold sweeps across forever ice, time itself seems frozen and human concerns mean nothing.

Our crew of five was out to climb and ski some of the most remote couloirs on the planet, but we quickly found –30°C temperatures would play a significant role. Pulling ski boots on in the morning was the first challenge; heating them with water bottles, we'd help each other pry them open to squeeze feet inside before the heat escaped. One day after leaving camp I made it only 50 metres before having to stop and swing my legs in a desperate bid to restore circulation; my feet were already frozen, while the 1,100-metre couloir we intended to ski on the edge of the Stewart Valley was still 18 kilometres distant.

Somehow I got there. Climbing up the massive corridor of rock was an otherworldly experience—as if the silver granite itself were serenading us. The echo of each breath, of crampons and ice axe digging into snow, felt like instruments in an orchestrated rhythm that rang with each step. Just you and the mountain, making music.

At the top of the final icy pitch we switched quickly to ski gear, knowing we needed to descend fast as the cold really set in. Dropping in was a long-awaited payoff, and the intensity of concentration took over the worry of potential frostbite, turn after careful turn until I raced out of the bottom in perfect snow and let out a hoot—a skier's expression of snowbound joy.

The high wore off quickly as we huddled at the base, sharing a cup of half-warm tea. Having not really felt them for more than eight hours, I voiced concern about my feet, though there was nothing to do but suck it up. Getting through the "Eye of the Tiger"—a phrase another photographer friend offered in such situations—gave me strength as I began the return trek.

A slow, very pink sunset lit the 1,200-metre walls of the Walker Citadel above camp, and I skinned towards the glow for hours. It presented one of the most beautiful photographs I could ever have taken in the mountains, but fear of losing my feet kept me from even thinking about stopping.

I spent the next five days in my sleeping bag, trying to bring two blackened toes back to life, armed with a loaded shotgun in case a polar bear wandered into camp. I was disappointed not to be out exploring further with the boys, but thankful to still have my feet.

I spent the next five days in my sleeping bag trying to bring two blackened toes back
to life, armed with a loaded shotgun in case a polar bear wandered into camp.

LEFT + RIGHT Photos by Jordan Manley.

LEFT Unnamed couloir on Baffin Island. Photo by Jordan Manley. **ABOVE** Art by Chad Sayers. **RIGHT** Photo by Jordan Manley.

Photo by Jordan Manley.

HEMU

Everything around us was sliding. We'd already hacked our way through two road-blocking avalanches and enthusiasm for our objective was withering; tensions grew as night approached.

Slithering through a canyon high above a half-frozen river, the string of vehicles in which we were embedded came to a halt at yet another five-metre-high mound of snow blocking the road: the mother of all slides—and it was fresh.

At first we hid in the truck, tucked under a small cliff. Others stood outside their vehicles, laughing and chain-smoking. *I am not gonna die here tonight* was all I could think. We got out and started shovelling, four hours straight, the constant echo of avalanches in the darkness a reminder we could be buried at any moment. And then it rained—shut down before we even started.

We'd come to ski the uncharted peaks of the Altai Mountains in Western China's Xinjiang province. This wild, isolated range—a collision on a map between China, Kazakhstan, Russia and Mongolia—was believed to be the birthplace of skiing.

Our arrival to the village of Hemu coincided with Chinese New Year, and locals welcomed us to their traditional celebration. Outside the venue, through billows of cigarette smoke, men on horseback playing tug-of-war with a goat offered us skeptical stares. Inside, children danced in colourful washes to tinny music leaking from old speakers. Women in beautiful dresses prepared the feast: an entire cow on a platter, guts and all. We'd already been sick—twice—and this was more questionable fare. We were starving, but terrified to eat.

Hemu itself bristled with contrasts: unbelievable views of surrounding peaks when the sun broke through, while on the streets mud-caked cows foraged in piles of garbage. Ultimately, a horse-drawn sled delivered at least one of our objectives: a few kilometres outside town we were able to film a Kazakhstani man crafting traditional wooden skis directly from a tree. Returning under the radiant light of a full moon, the sled driver suddenly mumbled something, threw me the reins, and jumped off. Alone, Manley and I sat dumbfounded as the massive horse galloped across flats, over hills, down embankments, into the trees and over an old slide path.

It was heading home, we reckoned, and would deliver us as well. But the raw beauty and isolation of the place took the edge off our uncertainty—a moment completely opposite from how the trip began.

LEFT • RIGHT Photos by Garrett Grove.

Steve Ogle at the Fitz Roy massif, Argentinian Patagonia. Photo by Chad Sayers.

PATAGONIA

From Day One we thought we might never make it.

It was October 2004, and three speechless young men stood where the Argentine Navy had dropped us—in an austere corner of Patagonia that our 20-year-old map showed as the toe of a glacier. But the glacier had since been replaced by a two-kilometre-wide lake, filled with enormous icebergs calved from its retreating face.

The opportunity to make a second journey to Patagonia had been a gift. I was fascinated by its landscapes, scale, emptiness and grandeur—the dark shadows cast by granite spires clawing tortured skies, the sharp reflections of peaks and clouds on turquoise lakes, and the endlessly circling condors, ever-watchful of your isolation and mortality. It would be my first real expedition—a 30-day, self-supported traverse of the Southern Patagonia Ice Field, with a plan to ski a few peaks along the way.

Like siege climbing, big traverses require a ton of gear, which usually means plenty of upward shuttling onto the ice where you can dump it all into a sled. This time it started with paddling loads across the iceberg lake for two days on a sketchy raft—built with wood and wire from an abandoned hut—hoping it didn't collapse beneath us, then making laps across three different glaciers before climbing up and over a crevassed 500-metre headwall onto the icecap proper.

On Day 11, nestled in our tent, we took comfort in our exhaustion: the hunger to ski unknown peaks was still strong and we were close to our main objectives. But the morning horizon held ominous black clouds, and by the time we returned from reconnaissance on a nearby col, the weather hit us full-on. Even for this infamously stormy part of the world, it was the storm of storms. As 100-km/h winds tore at vulnerable nylon walls, waves of anxiety consumed us—*How much could the tent take?* Fear of being buried alive and never found was real as we dug out the tent in shifts.

After 10 straight days shovelling against the storm and getting low on food, we made the call to retreat. We set our compass due east and spun whatever sliver of hope we held for skiing in the direction of survival. Roped together in a whiteout, trapped in a maze of ice, we descended by intuition onto the labyrinthine Perito Moreno Glacier, whose perilously fractured surface is considered a natural wonder of the world. Navigating from one steep, exposed ice ridge to another, crossing bottomless crevasses on fragile snow bridges, we trusted each other implicitly. At one point, clinging to a teetering serac with both ice axes, skis A-framed on my 40-kilo pack and camera strapped to my chest, I caught my reflection in blue ice; it was the first time I actually saw myself as a man, an alpine warrior smiling into the face of wild adversity. I felt that if I got through this I could survive anything.

A break in the weather on Day 28 delivered a sighting of land from our storm-tossed sea of ice—and a chance to escape. We pushed hard, now hungry and somewhat delirious. Despite the ever-present danger there was also a sense of freedom in wandering such an unforgiving landscape with friends, completely at the mercy of the elements—a Zen lesson, had we been aware, on what it meant to find beauty in suffering.

Two days later we lay on solid ground, cherishing the feel and smell of dirt as we tried to gather strength after four days without food. Suddenly, the improbable odour of cooking meat reached our nostrils. In our starving state, were we hallucinating? Investigating, the smell proved real, and we were welcomed to the campfire of a group of Argentine guides who were feasting on roast lamb. It felt surreal, given what we'd just endured, that not only had we made it out alive, but somehow found a hot meal.

LEFT Photo by Kari Medig. **RIGHT** Torres del Paine National Park, Chilean Patagonia. Photo by Steve Ogle.

It started with paddling loads across the iceberg lake for two days on a sketchy raft built with wood and wire from an abandoned hut, hoping it didn't collapse beneath us.

LEFT Photo by Steve Ogle. **RIGHT** Perito Moreno Glacier, Argentinian Patagonia. Art by L. Barnes.

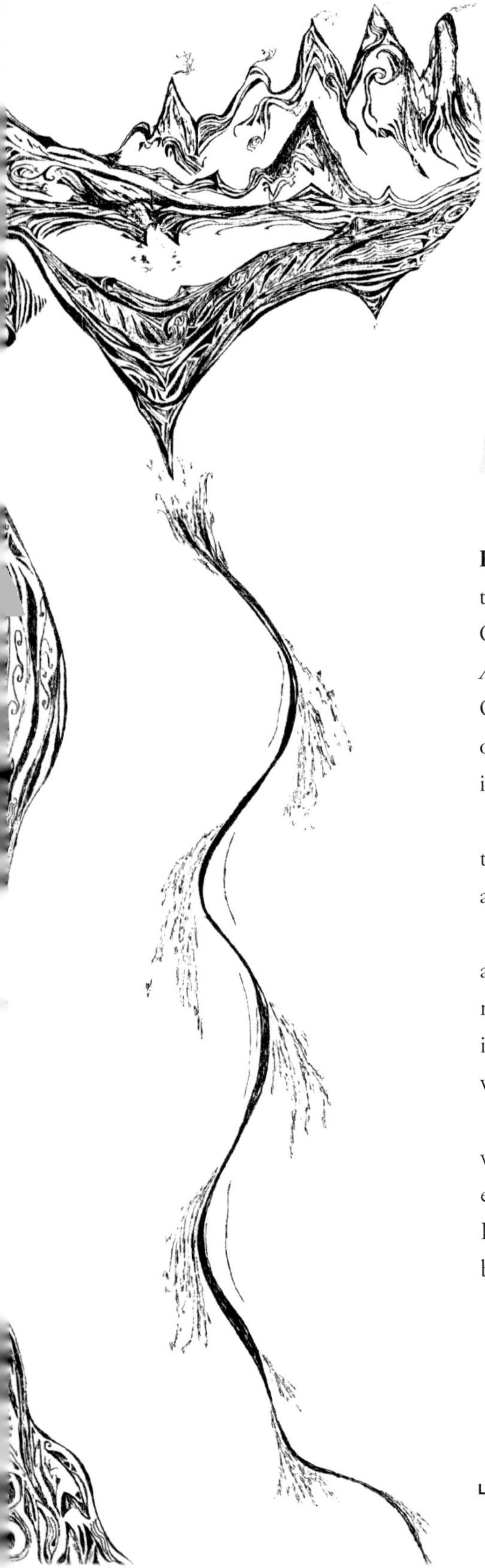

ALASKA

Returning from the difficult Kashmir trip, I had looked forward to taking time off to heal. Once home, however, Whistler-based Sherpas Cinema invited me to Haines, Alaska, to shoot the final segment of *All.I.Can,* a feature-length film that would go on to win many awards. Given my long-held dream of being in a major ski film, and recognizing the opportunity to work with world-renowned cinematographers, it was impossible to say no.

And then there was Alaska. From an early age I'd seen this frontier as the ultimate ski experience, yearning for a chance to ski its celebrated lines and fluted spines with the kind of style and grace I'd seen in so many photos.

I walked the empty streets of Haines on a cold, crisp evening, admiring distant peaks that sailed over rooftops. This was surely the fulfillment of another dream, yet I was still injured and fearful about my ability; in an honest conversation with myself, I acknowledged that I wasn't fit but would still give it everything I had. It should have been a warning.

Four weather days later, the helicopter lifted off with three skiers, and we warmed up on a few shorter lines to feel out the snow. Conditions were excellent. We headed towards a 400-metre wall called the Japan Spines. From the back of the chopper my sightlines weren't great, but I could see a big fracture from an old avalanche and that there was very little fresh snow left on which three skiers might find fresh lines—perhaps another sign I should pass. We circled again before unloading on a knife-edge ridge, the most radical heli-drop I've ever experienced.

We hacked through a cornice to get onto the face, where it was determined that I would ski last. When my turn came, I kick-turned into position for the countdown and was shocked to see I'd have to drop six metres onto 50-degree hardpack. The radio crackled that cameras would roll in 15 seconds. My heart pounded; it was another moment I'd waited years for, yet I was facing a line my gut told me not to ski.

I stuck the landing and traversed around a rocky corner above the line I intended to ski. Looking down, I charged off the top into the void. It was steep, sloughing all around me and happening fast. On my first turn I hit the north side of the spine and powder exploded into the sky, but when I crossed back in the other direction the spine was rock hard from the earlier avalanche, and with my weak leg I couldn't control the forces trying to toss me.

I almost recovered, but ended up cartwheeling down the entire face, unsure where I was until I launched over a bergschrund near the bottom and came to a halt. I knew right away I'd blown my knee but there was some small consolation: I should have been dead.

LEFT Art by Chad Sayers. **RIGHT** A peak near Haines, Alaska, USA. Photo by Oskar Enander.

LEFT Skiing to the water's edge in Norway. Photo by Mattias Fredriksson. **RIGHT** Accessing ski descents by kayak in the Westfjords, Iceland. Photo by Jordan Manley.

Photo by Jordan Manley.

La Grave

SECTION V

LEFT • RIGHT Photos by Jordan Manley.

Photo by Jordan Manley.

SHIFT

One tranquil evening, cradling a cup of tea on my porch in Whistler, a voice within me spoke in what felt like desperation: *Why don't you just move to La Grave for the winter?*

I didn't hesitate in answering.

A shift in the rhythm I'd been living made sense. During seemingly endless missions chasing storms around the world and filming for *A Skier's Journey,* I had accumulated injury after injury. Short off-seasons of only a few months didn't deliver enough time to fully heal, and the compounded chronic pain had become almost too much to bear. My body felt shattered, and along with it, sadly, my will to ski.

The isolated village of La Grave in the southern French Alps had always beckoned for a longer stay. From my first visit—inspired by an image in *Powder* magazine of American skier Doug Coombs traversing the heinously steep Pan de Rideau—I felt I would live there one day. And in that moment on my porch in Whistler, it seemed the perfect place to seek the kind of solace and inspiration I needed to continue skiing.

The move to the Alps would indeed bring light into my soul, but it would also usher in one of the darkest periods of my life.

LEFT Photo by Jordan Manley. **RIGHT** Pan de Rideau, La Grave, France. Photo by Guillaume Le Guillou.

The most unexpected yet
heartfelt moments always
seem to come into our lives
when the spirit is searching
for answers and longing
for inspiration.

LEFT Photo by Jordan Manley. **RIGHT** Banane Couloir, La Grave, France. Photo by Jordan Manley.

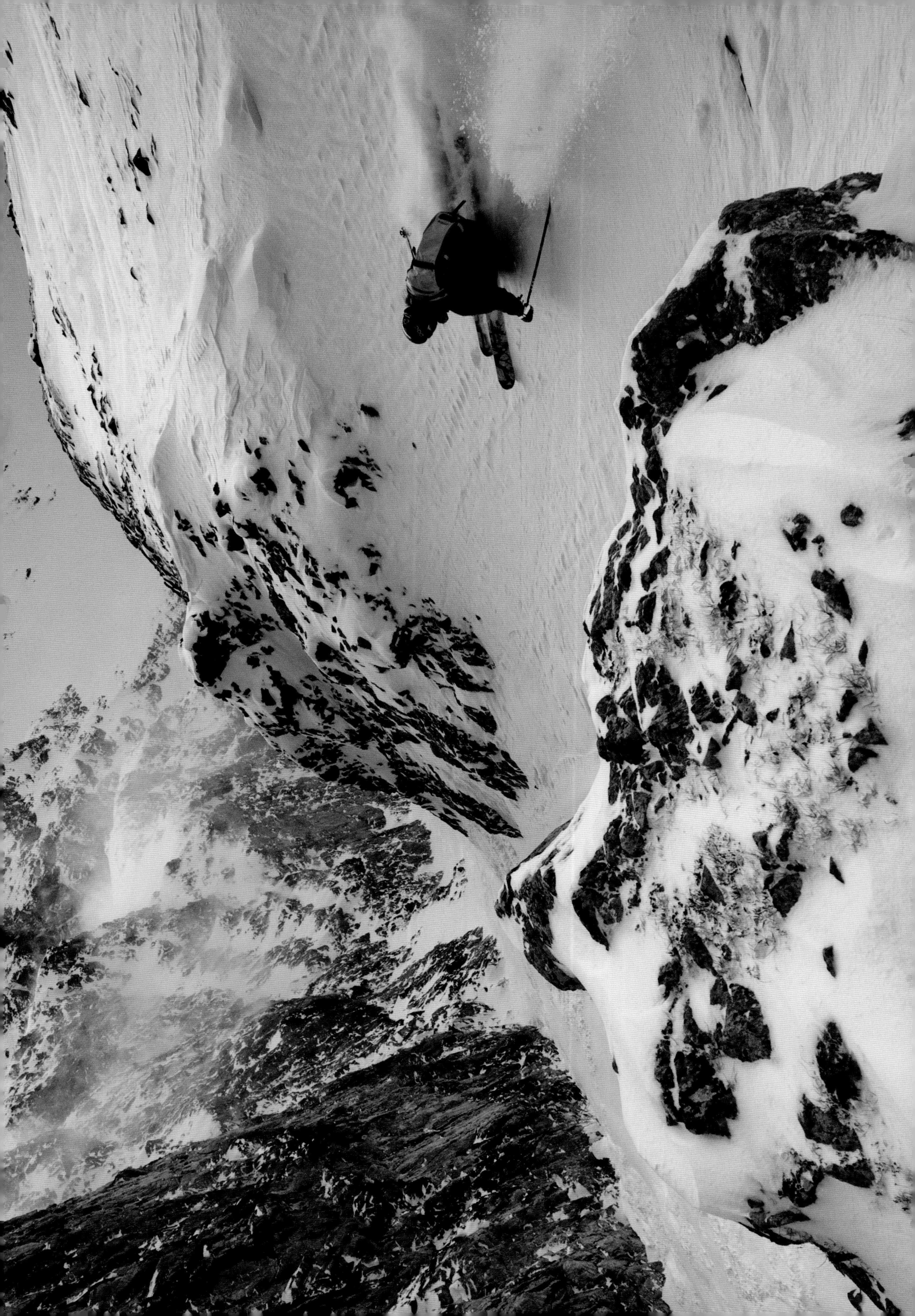

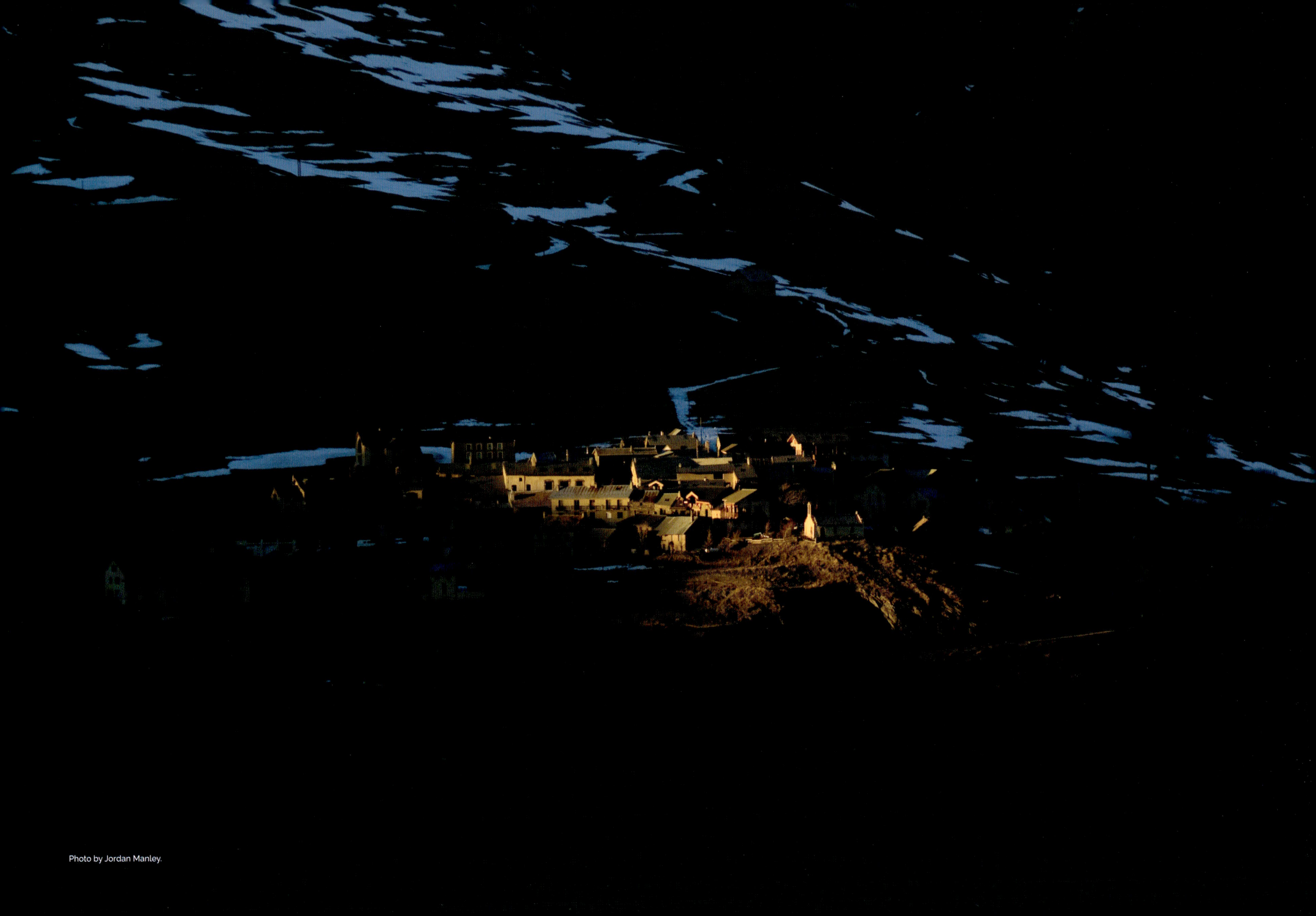

Photo by Jordan Manley.

VENTELON

Walking the empty, cobblestoned streets of Ventelon for the first time, I immediately felt the return of my ski spirit. This village of only fifty souls, perched fifteen switchbacks above La Grave, felt minuscule compared to the windswept glaciers hanging 2,000 metres above it on the legendary ski mountain of La Meije—it was easy to see from its elevated vantage how exposed, unpredictable and humbling that peak truly was. With La Grave poised to be the arena that saved my skiing, it seemed the perfect base.

I rented a quaint loft apartment in a 16th-century stone house—apropos given that everything else in Ventelon seemed to have paused in time around the same era. The town's pace was conducive to savouring an espresso, making time for conversation, walking instead of driving. Above all, folks lived the same ethos as the valley's earliest settlers: with a passion for the mountains.

While I shared much adventure in La Grave with many amazing friends, I also spent a significant chunk of time keeping to myself. I could take in an unobstructed view of La Meije through a set of French doors to my balcony. On clear, star-filled nights I'd lie on the heated brick floor, gazing through a skylight; other times I'd watch candlelight flicker on the ceiling as I embraced the sound of storms that sometimes raged for days. The seclusion was exactly what I craved.

When the weather calmed enough, I'd ski down to the village through winter's raw howl, sliding down streets, dipping through alleyways, passing locals tending livestock as the smell of home fires, swirling in the chaos of wind, delivered a strange sense of comfort.

For a while, this was home.

I love getting to the lift first thing in the morning after a storm, when the sky is clearing and the trees are full of snow, seeing the same folks drinking their tea and smoking half-hash joints while waiting on word of conditions up high.

LEFT Photo by Mattias Fredriksson. **RIGHT** Photo by Jordan Manley.

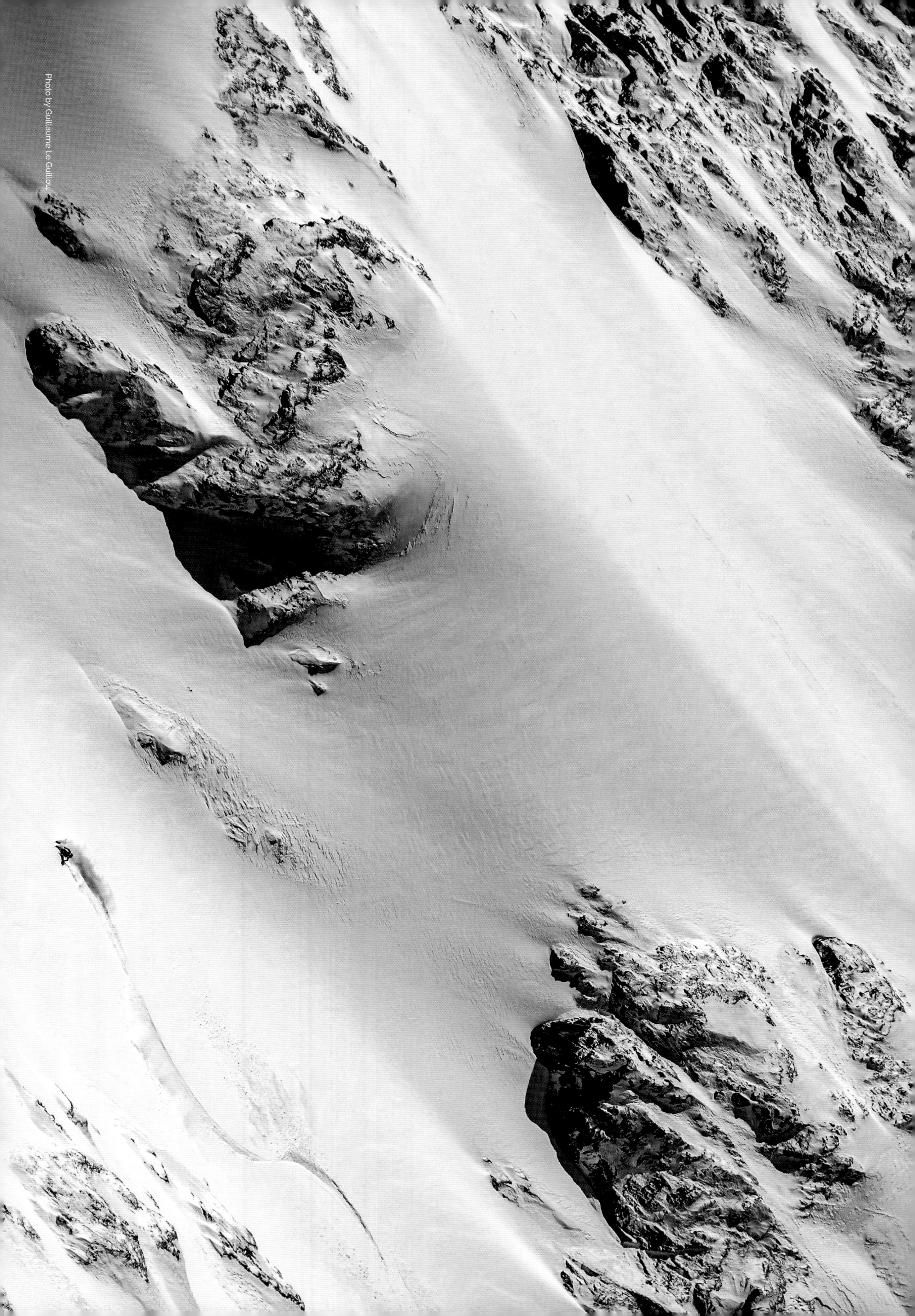

Photo by Guillaume Le Guillou

UNLEASHED

Le téléphérique—an odd, pulse-style cable car with groups of five gondolas linked together—was the means to gain 2,100 metres of vertical from the village of La Grave. At the summit station, a 360-degree view took in the peaks of Belledonne, Thabor and Aravis, as well as the Mont Blanc massif. A few steps farther put you atop the Girose Glacier and myriad potential descents.

Uncontrolled and unpatrolled, there were no signs in La Grave marking cliffs or rocks, just a civil demand that you have your backcountry wits about you: if you weren't competent enough to rescue yourself in the event it became necessary, or you hadn't hired a guide, you had no right stepping into your skis.

I learned much about these mountains from the phenomenal souls with whom I shared memorable days: Canadian expat Ptor Spricenieks, American ski guide Joe Vallone, Swedish ripper Lars Krantz and my cherished friend Josefine, mother of two and wife of local guide Per Ås.

We sailed through the mountains and surfed between the walls of endless couloirs, hearts pumping, breathing hard, ever-present in the quest to stay upright. Diving from snow pocket to snow pocket, dodging crevasses, disappearing into powder explosions—popping out with just enough time to set a mark for the next safe turn before vanishing again. Skiing La Grave was a soul dance, your partner the ever-present possibility of death.

When these mountains spoke, it was imperative that you listened. Sometimes the messages were obvious—a massive avalanche ripping down the face of La Meije, or a serac breaking off a glacier as you skied by. Other times it was more a whisper in the midst of a storm, or while stuck in the crux on a wind-hammered traverse, thinking of all who'd died before us on this ledge, peering down at the same exposed rocks.

Was it faith, fear or skiing with an intuitive heart that kept us alive? None of us was sure, but I learned fast that if you didn't respect this sacred place, you weren't long for this world.

CRUX

While La Grave was good for my soul, other forces were conspiring to take me down.

Scanning my weathered skin and wrinkled face, I saw the ravages of the elements etched in the mirror, as well as the ongoing pain from years of self-inflicted injury. That young, fresh-faced skier from SilverStar had disappeared and I wondered who I had become.

Mistreatment had brought my body to a point that I often couldn't walk to the téléphérique without my left leg screaming *Go home before something terrible happens!* Yet I continued to prioritize skiing above other forms of happiness or comfort that could free me from the turmoil—such as my girlfriend at the time. We'd met in the surf in Costa Rica, and had been riding out the usual romantic ripples of a long-distance relationship. We spent months in the tropics together in the off-season and she had visited La Grave a few times. Like any partnership, it demanded attention, more than I was willing to offer up at times, because skiing was everything to me. Or at least I believed so.

Just like the early days on Blackcomb Mountain, starting at the top and stopping at the bottom was my jam here. No standing around or pausing halfway. Just going fast, accelerating in the difficult spots, navigating by instinct. While my ongoing physical discomfort was tempered by the adrenaline of descent, it always surged back when I stopped, often crippling me to the point that I would only make it as far as the floor of my apartment, where I might then lie for hours. My mind felt clear with so much space in which to be still, but my body was overwhelmed, confused and tired.

And of course I was still a working pro, expected to be available when asked. In preparation for out-of-town film trips, I'd slip into one of the stone troughs near the church, ancient vessels that overflowed with ice-cold water from the mountains. The deep resonance of the church bells brought serenity while the water numbed my body—along with swirling yin-yang thoughts of skiing for the cameras again. I dreaded having to leave La Grave to "work" at skiing, though staying wasn't supporting my healing either.

Was it just the issue of physical injuries, or was my body also starting to reflect this inner conflict? Whichever it might be, it was reshaping the cadence of my descents, and the harsh reality was that for the first time in an 11-year career, I was literally fighting to stay on my feet. I knew I couldn't stick to this routine, but I also couldn't find it in me to walk away.

Photo by Daniel Ronnback

I'm thinking about the
many blissful walks
up the switchbacks
under a full moon,
the glow of the spring
sky, midnight wanders
with foxes and rabbits
leading me home.

LEFT Photo by Jordan Manley. **RIGHT** Photo by Mattias Fredriksson.

RECKONING

"It's *over*!" Her words rang in my ear through the phone. Our love hadn't been strong enough to survive the long stretches of separation, and I couldn't give up skiing to move to the tropics.

After weeks of emotional anguish, I woke up one morning and decided to ski a La Grave classic with a few friends—a 2,150-metre couloir-studded run that included a technical rappel 1,400 metres downslope of the entrance. Conditions were in top form: a cold, tight snowpack with 15 centimetres of fresh snow on top. Taking the lead, I dropped in but skied haltingly, scared to let the surface snow run. Off balance and riding the tails of my skis, physically drained from overthinking and not sleeping, nothing felt quite right. Yet this mission had been meant to heal all that ailed me—to literally save my soul.

The top section skied well, but as I descended towards a large rock concealing the rappel anchor, I realized the couloir had frozen up. Soon it became too dangerous to ski, and I began to carefully sidestep my way towards the anchor, now 100 metres below. Unroped, at each downward step I plugged a finger into the hard snow as a lifeline until, 10 metres from the rock, the snow met blue ice. A fall here meant a 600-metre death ride. Was I going to try and be the hero or listen to intuition and sidestep back up? It was a defining moment.

So, God, I thought. *What do you think of this one?*

The only answer was the sound of my breathing.

Gingerly, I stepped out on the ice. Sure enough, my ski slid out and I was left dangling by a finger. Though I'd had no intention of going for it, and would, in fact, sidestep up to build a new anchor where we could lower ourselves to the main anchor and safely navigate the couloir's crux, I had needed to experience the feeling that I wasn't in control of my life, my mind or the path ahead—the stark line between the end of everything or the chance at a new beginning. And in that moment, I knew: I had to hang up my skis, get out of town and sort myself out.

Rappelling into the La Voute Couloir, La Grave, France.
Photo by Jordan Manley.

Photo by Mattias Fredriksson.

Broken

SECTION VI

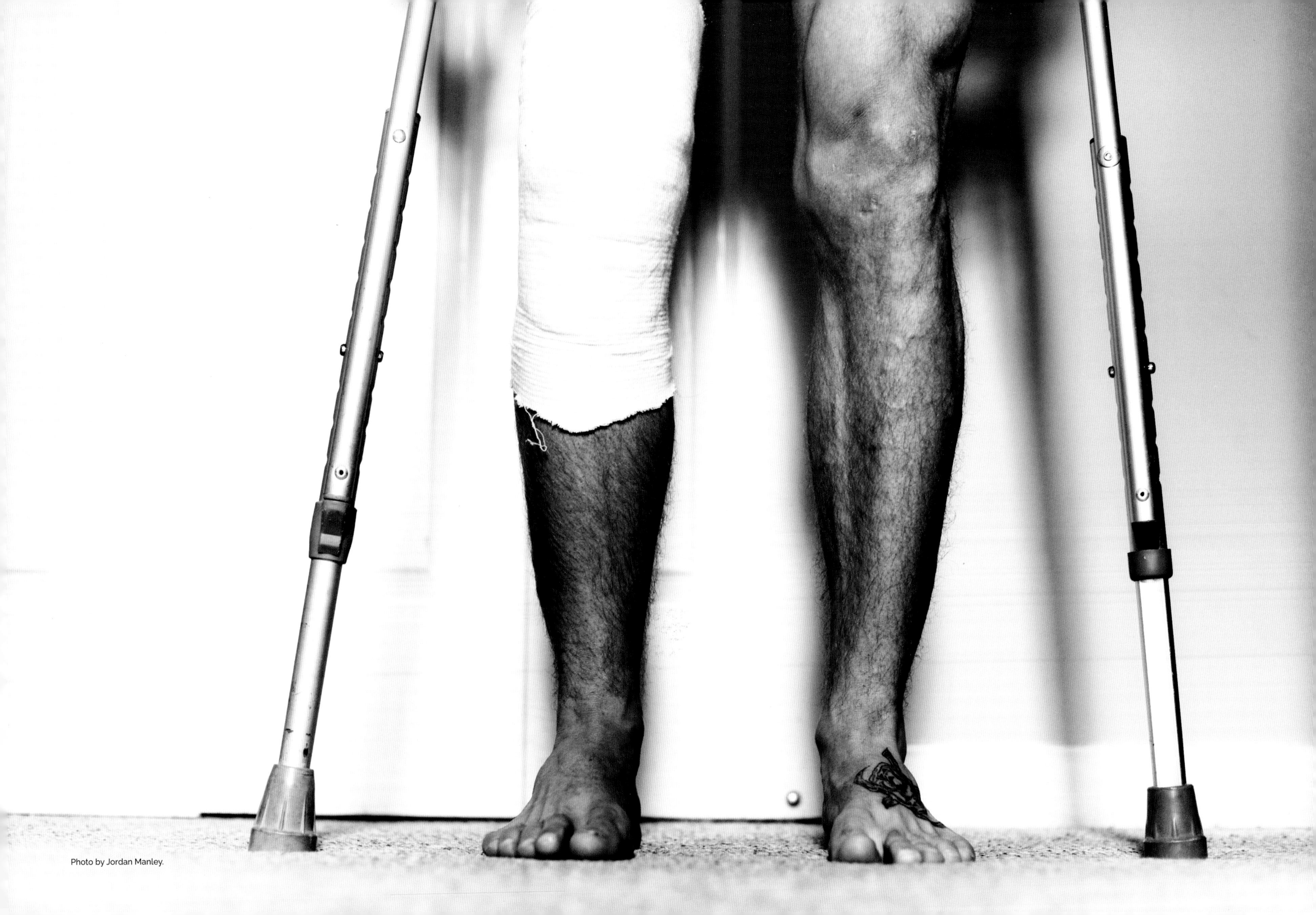

Photo by Jordan Manley.

LOST

Mountains show no mercy to the weak, and I was humbly shown the door that day in the couloir.

Losing the girl had extinguished the only remaining tendrils of light seeping into my life. Though I deserved it, the rejection stripped me of my self-esteem. Now emotionally raw on top of chronic physical pain, I saw clearly how unbalanced I had become. My attitude had shifted to insecurity, impatience and unpredictability—a dangerous combination in the mountains.

As the love dissolved, the warnings my body had been conveying for years grew louder: *stop skiing*. It was as if the pain now gushing from my heart was pooling in my feet, knees and legs, reminding me not only of my many injuries, but also the subtler yet steady wear on all of my joints.

In hindsight, I'm disturbed by how hard I kept training and pushing myself to travel and work as a pro skier when I could barely even stand, allowing for the overstimulation of everything else witnessed in those travels to gnaw at my fragility. Was I unconsciously administering some twisted, masochistic punishment for my hubris?

The departure from La Grave was dark and cold, full of tears and uncertainty for reasons I didn't yet understand. In a snowstorm, I packed up the car I'd leased from a friend of a friend, paid off my aged landlord and left town without a sound. Delirious and disoriented, I dropped the car in Chamonix and took a shuttle to the Geneva airport.

At this point, the only reasonable thing I could think to do was re-enter the nomadic world of self-discovery I'd left to become a pro. It wasn't clear that going home—or anything else—would achieve that: I had officially arrived at being totally lost.

LEFT • RIGHT Photos by Jordan Manley.

En route to Ushguli, Georgia. Photo by Jason Thompson.

REFLECTION

Lost, of course, was relative. During these difficult years I had felt that if I took a break from skiing, my lifestyle—my career—would end. Looking back, it wasn't the ego of recognition or status that drove me, but a heart clinging to a youthful dream it was reluctant to give up. Most professional athletes can relate: you go until you simply can't anymore.

The non-stop whirlwind of travel had also burdened me with an overload of emotional reality: the machinations of life in some of the most overpopulated and polluted cities in the world; the rate at which we were destroying the planet for money, control and attention; the extreme poverty, starvation and violence characterizing many places; and, of course, my undeniable role in all of it as a frequent traveller, as a consumer and even as a skier. Each of these realizations shook me to the core, frightening yet ultimately shaping me. At times, my inability to reconcile the world's indescribable beauty with its similarly indescribable suffering caused me to turn inward, unable to communicate my own juxtaposition of pain and joy.

Humbling experiences in far-flung locales often cradled me back, however briefly, to believing everything was actually OK, that I should simply be grateful for my own charmed and privileged life and the gift of being able to continue—despite how it was literally and figuratively crippling me. It was one such moment that finally brought about a much-needed watershed.

Years before, on a three-day layover in New Delhi with a film crew, I broke free of the group one night—as was becoming commonplace—to wallow in my inner turmoil. Sitting on the curb of a sidestreet with its own tumult of traffic, people and animals, I sipped a chai, praying to God to show me how I could possibly continue; by this point, I'd basically been skiing on one leg for five years. Amidst the cacophony and blurring lights, a figure caught my eye—a man dragging himself by his arms across the road. Cars and motorbikes swerved around him without any concern as he clawed his way forward. *Fuck—this guy doesn't even have any legs and I'm sitting here complaining to myself about mere pain.*

After this moment of awakening, I slowly began my own crawl from a self-made storm of despair.

I've tried to get by in this challenging time through sincere conversations with God, but I seem to be losing my connection with spirit. I'm torturing myself, really. I keep making the choice to put myself in all these situations. Things need to change.

LEFT Photo by Jordan Manley. **RIGHT** La Thuile ski area, Italy. Photo by Mattias Fredriksson.

LEFT Photo by Daniel Ronnback. **RIGHT** Mt. Baker ski area, Washington, USA. Photo by Jordan Manley.

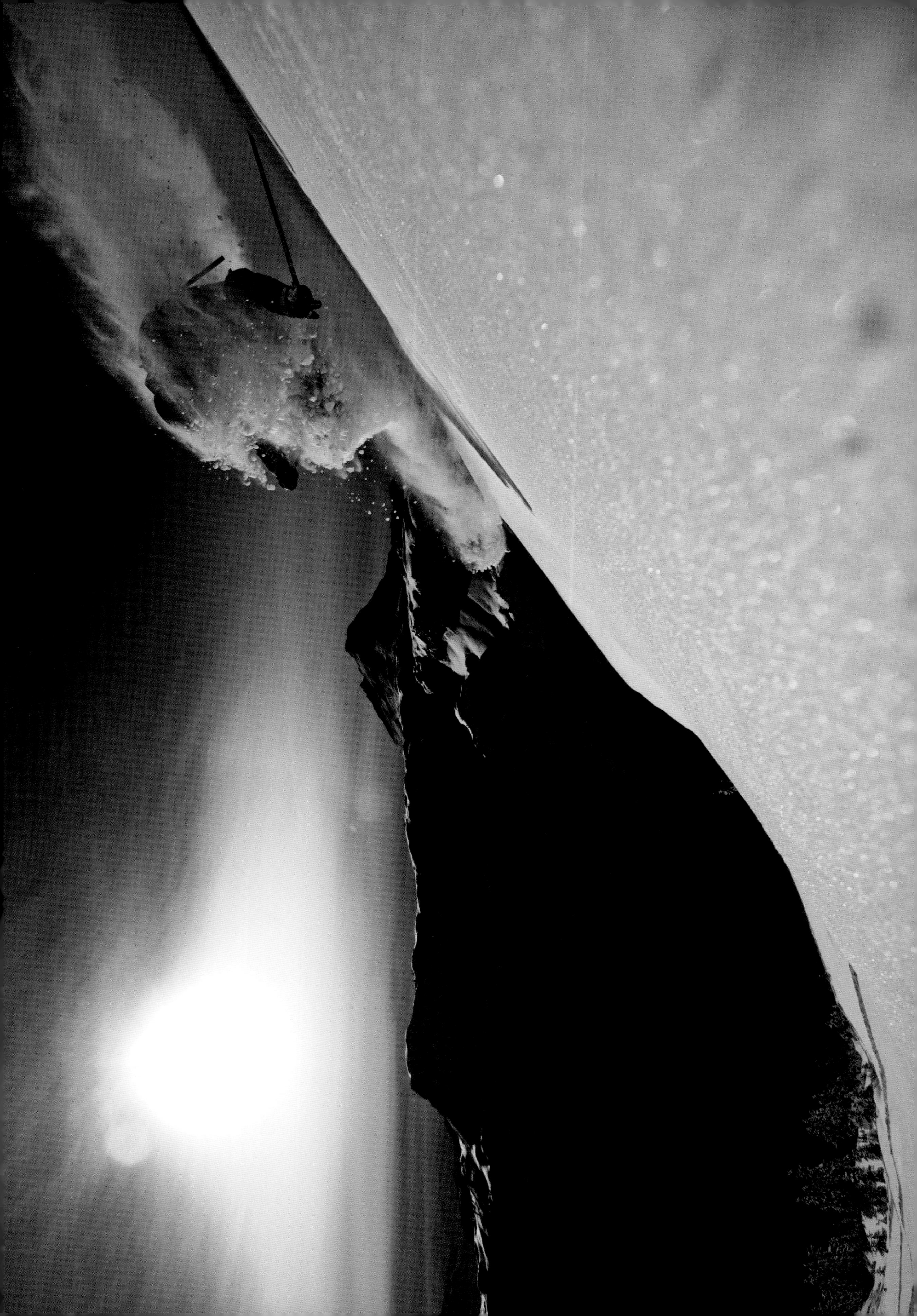

HEALING

To be broken was inevitable. Deep down I had always known that. So had others. One of five physiotherapists who worked on my injuries over this time stated the obvious: *Chad, maybe you should consider doing nothing for a few years so your body can heal.*

She had a point. My attempt to continue as a professional skier had reached a level of absurdity where I might ski half a day then take 10 days off; or go on a 20–30-day expedition, suffer constantly, and require years to incrementally overcome the damage.

Injuries and discomfort are familiar to any high-level athlete. But for me it wasn't just the transient cold feet or occasional sore knees most skiers experience. The permanent reminders of a broken femur, multiple blown knees and feet I could no longer feel represented an insidious cycle: get injured, have surgery, train back via gym time and physiotherapy, learn to trust the body again, start skiing again, coax the mind past mental hurdles again, load the injury to a high level of impact again, then put it all on the line… *again.*

Staying in the game required that you invest—often tens of thousands of dollars—in the fragile vessel that carried your soul and kept you performing.

After Kashmir I wasn't much interested in pharmaceutical remedies. Part of me came to believe that if I couldn't feel the actual pain, it was dangerous to use that body part. Thus, in desperation I would surrender to strangers and treatments that offered any prospect of relief—yoga, intramuscular stimulation, craniosacral therapy, massage, acupuncture, reiki. Over the years I would let an Indonesian man with a clove cigarette bobbing in his mouth walk all over me on the bamboo floor of a thatched hut, undergo 60 hours of myofascial release under a palm tree in Costa Rica, and try to soak away the torment in everything from Icelandic geothermal pools to traditional Japanese *onsens*, from public bathhouses in Iran to hot springs in the Honduran jungle.

No matter what I tried, however, nothing offered more than temporary relief. Eventually, I realized there was only one thing that could truly address the deepest levels of physical misery: myself.

Photo by Jordan Manley.

LEFT • RIGHT Photos by Jordan Manley.

All photos in this section by Chad Sayers unless otherwise noted.

Traveller

SECTION VII

WAVES

What happened in the couloir in La Grave frightened me, but it was only one of many close calls and crucial bad decisions that had to be given voice, analyzed and acted upon.

During the flight back to Canada from Geneva, I was in a fugue state. Ditto the next three weeks. I ended up at a friend's place in Whistler staring at the walls, too jet-lagged and confused to even eat—something I rarely had trouble with. Self-questioning swirled. Did a heartbreak *really* drive me from the Alps? Was it my nature to let relationships get the best of me? Was I losing my grip on reality? What about my ski career? And going home—*seriously?*

The truth had a much blunter edge: my career pursuits had finally brought me to my knees on every front. Everything else was just a result.

Finding myself back in Whistler was the fitting beginning of a long rebirthing process—yet one I had no idea I was entering, and thus no way of knowing it would eventually lead me back to the mountains. I didn't stay long. I couldn't let people see me in the state I was in and I definitely didn't want to ski. I needed a new path, one that could both reignite my love for travel away from the alpine heights and also aid my healing.

That path would be a parallel trail I'd been following for a while: surfing.

LEFT Dalwhinnie Distillery, Scotland. Photo by Bruno Long.

Itacaré, Brazil.

GOOD LUCK
Cubana

Balangan, Indonesia.

INDONESIA

I'll always remember the day I found out what a proper set wave looked—and felt—like.

Two friends and I were in Nias off the west coast of Sumatra, an island whose right-breaking wave was rated one of the planet's best. It was my first-ever surf trip, the start of a new obsession and prelude to many trips to Indonesia. At the time, most of what I knew of surfing was what I'd seen on TV—pro surfers like Kelly Slater and Andy Irons, charging fearlessly down the line deep inside a perfect barrel. As with skiing, I was drawn to something that looked so pure and free.

Nias wasn't easy to reach in the late nineties. Civil unrest made for difficult navigation in the port town of Sibolga, and transportation was a challenge: reaching Nias took 15 hours, battling seasickness on a muggy, listing ferry that seemed likely to sink, surrounded by people smoking, snoring, sobbing and puking. At least accommodation was cheap: a basic hut in front of the famous wave was only four dollars a night. We slept on handmade wooden beds draped in mosquito nets to protect from malaria and dengue fever.

We had been posted up a month, our days filled with swaying in hammocks, scanning for waves and collecting shells while dining on homemade veggie burgers, tropical fruit and fresh coconut milk. We also enjoyed the local habits of drinking strong Indo coffee and puffing on clove cigarettes. And we surfed. As much as our 50-cents-a-day rental boards could handle. Near the trip's end, paddling out on what seemed an average-sized day, a wall of water suddenly appeared on the horizon. As it raced towards me, growing in size and menace, I froze in fear. At the last second, I decided to paddle at it, scratching at the water's surface with every ounce of energy I possessed to make it over. But I didn't. A solid three-metre bomb unloaded right on my head.

The blow was so strong it felt like my limbs were being torn off. Churned inside the washing machine, I bounced off the reef, was picked up again by the rotation of the wave, and spun back into the dark green maelstrom. The pattern continued for a while. Finally, as the last molecule of oxygen was squeezed from my lungs, I popped up with just enough time to inhale another breath before the next wave replayed the whole ordeal.

Eventually, gulping air, I washed up on the reef. Terrified by the beating but grateful to be alive, I picked up my battered surfboard and made my way to the beach—only to be greeted by a gaggle of kids who found high comedy in the *bule* (foreigner) being hammered by the Indian Ocean. Where their larger-than-life smiles were usually welcome, that day they snuffed out the last of my dignity.

After spontaneously packing for a surf trip to Indonesia's Mentawai Islands, and then five days of travel, I stepped off an overnight ferry at sunrise. Locals paddled me through mangrove swamps in a handcrafted canoe to a surf camp on the northern tip of Masokut island. That afternoon I surfed a nearby A-frame peak. It felt exciting to be back in these crystal waters but, as always, a little nerve-wracking surfing the powerful Indian Ocean over shallow reefs. Rinsing off in the shower that night, a different kind of wave washed over my body—a debilitating fatigue as if I'd been hit by a truck. I almost passed out, but managed to crawl into bed before being overtaken by sweats, chills, and fever. I spent the next week hallucinating by candlelight as a bout of dengue fever—acquired en route—took me under.

DATANG
LAPANGAN
RANGGO
16

ARTCO

KALALAU

After an 18-kilometre hike along Kauai's Na Pali Coast, I reached the end of the Kalalau Valley Trail. Staring across the beach, I envisioned the first humans to arrive here in outrigger sailing dugouts around 1200 AD. They'd navigated 3,200 kilometres of ocean from Polynesia using only stars and the wind as guides. This beach had been one of the birthplaces of Hawaiian culture.

I ultimately made seven solo trips into the sacred valley of Kalalau, hiking in via the rugged trail or kayaking, depending how my legs felt after the ski season. No other single location helped more with my physical healing, nor my mind: I could sit in caves near the beach, meditating to clear my thoughts and restore balance.

I first fell in love with the island of Kauai—its surfing and its people—before succumbing to the call of Kalalau, which drew its own distinct brand of seekers and sirens. My memories are filled with fires on the beach, angelic singing and romantic encounters that brought silhouettes dancing across the rocks, smiles sparkling in the starlight and nights spent on bluffs high above the crashing sea.

Kalalau's surreal landscape of jagged, green mountains was similarly magic. I'd dream of the peaks covered in snow, of skiing down their flanks. I was easily seduced by the peaceful rhythm of a life where you could wander beaches naked, cool your browning skin in freshwater pools, chase rainbows into the canyon with a camera and be lulled to sleep under trees by an orchestra of waterfalls and birdsong. Each piece opened my mind to the power of this place; following footpaths through ancient fruit groves and abandoned homesteads of the original Hawaiian settlers, I heard whispers in the breeze and felt the presence of spirits.

On one trip at the beginning of the rainy season, I forged deeper into the valley, hoping not to see anyone. I arrived late in the afternoon in poor weather; it was dark and windy, with an uneasy energy building. I dropped my pack, made a small fire and put up the tarp.

My first mistake—as mosquitoes would later attest—was not bringing a tent; my second was camping in the forest instead of on the bluffs. Sitting cross-legged and a little stoned in my sleeping bag, I lit the stove to prepare dinner. Suddenly the wind picked up, carrying the sound of nearby thunder and lightning strikes. Seconds later, a massive tree branch snapped off and landed directly beside me, sending the dinner pot flying as I stared, frozen in shock.

Though I felt truly free in this otherworldly paradise, it was a reminder that I was still on Earth—where the law of gravity and other cautions applied.

My memories are filled with fires on the beach,
angelic singing and romantic encounters that
brought silhouettes dancing across the rocks,
smiles sparkling in the starlight and nights
spent on bluffs high above the crashing sea.

HONDURAS

The White Palace is what I called the house my parents built on Isla Roatán, 50 kilometres off the coast of Honduras. Perched on a hill with a circling view of sparkling reefs and crystal-blue waters, it felt like the setting of an out-of-time romantic mystery. It was easy to see why they hadn't hesitated in leaving British Columbia to start a new life here.

Once they took up residence, I'd typically head to the island for a couple months each spring. With no agenda, I was free to wander the beaches and lose myself in sea and sky. Diving on part of the Belize Barrier Reef, the world's second-largest reef system, I began to understand more about ocean life. At night I lay on my back in the garden, tracking starry heavens framed by palms that swayed in the island's strong easterlies. After a tough winter, the tropical shift offered a chance to ponder everything from the universe to personal questions.

The beauty of Roatán came with a price: tropical storms, malaria, the local influence of drugs and alcohol, and murder and theft associated with violent gangs all spoke to a swirling darkness. As the island's tourism grew, the influx of money came with an inevitable increase in crime. In such impoverished areas, it was understandably easy to confuse the idea of obtaining wealth by whatever means with a better way of life. With the island changing fast, my parents quite suddenly decided to sell. Three weeks later they were on the Honduran mainland, wondering what was next.

This time they built on the edge of Pico Bonito National Park, set between mountains and sea, surrounded by rainforest brimming with a diverse flora and fauna. The *Sayers Wellness Centre,* as this home was dubbed, became a sanctuary not just for myself, but many friends and fellow travellers.

Photography was an obsession during my visits. I could easily lose myself in the jungle with only my Nikon, a tripod and a few rolls of film, or spend time capturing the energy of local kids playing in afternoon light, the quiet shadows of palms reaching across the sand or the telltale story of broken concrete constellated by bullet holes. An old man sitting in a rocking chair with a bible, or an ill person who'd requested to breathe their last breath on the green steps of a white church—capturing these images became a form of self-expression that also spoke to the reverence I experienced as I witnessed them. Though my photographs didn't feel intrusive, I had to be careful. At times I found myself in too deep with an aggressive person, or overstayed a self-imposed sundown curfew; you could easily get your throat slit here if you crossed the wrong lines.

As I had learned from the mountains, the more you expose yourself to danger, the more likely something might happen. For my parents, the growing lawlessness and perils of the country—friends killed, the unnerving knowledge that at any moment gangsters with AK-47s could break down their door—was wearing their tolerance thin. A letter written in blood and laid on their doorstep demanding $25,000 or death erased all notion of continuing a peaceful life here.

But they couldn't leave. Feeling trapped during the five long years required to sell the second house, they thrived and grew together in that time—an expression of unconditional love amidst the uncertainty. Despite their eventual exit, my parents' faith and adventurous spirits had gifted our family 12 memorable years in the Caribbean.

Sambo Creek on the Caribbean coast of Honduras.

Sunrises and sunsets have been a big part of my photography, seeming to mark the beginning or end of something profound and often romantic in my travels. I have countless memories of running frantically down empty beaches with my tripod, hoping to capture that last bit of light. Eventually I realized I was so caught up in looking through the viewfinder that I was missing the experience. The novelty of chasing sunsets gave way to sitting on the sand in stillness and appreciating the wonders of light and colour.

Left to right, Susan, Doug, Carrie and Chad Sayers at "The White Palace" on Roatán, Honduras.

Spending time with my family has always been important. Seeing them change over the years and accepting their evolving views isn't always easy, but I'm sure they could say the same about me.

Taj Mahal, Agra, India.

INDIA

At some point as a teenager, I swapped my dream of a hockey career with a desire to become a *National Geographic* photographer, documenting the faces and places of the world. Later, as a pro skier, I honoured that whim by investing every penny made from the industry into travelling and shooting photos, chasing the light and unique experiences of each new setting. In 2008 the search brought me to India.

Trying to pack as much as possible into a month, I watched the fire of a rising sun fill the sky behind the Taj Mahal, slept under the stars in Rajasthan and rode camelback for 100 kilometres through sand dunes in the Thar Desert. Cramming into a steamy, second-class train cabin with barely enough room to breathe, I watched colourful landscapes through the window on a 24-hour journey to the beaches of Goa. Along the way, I photographed anything that caught my eye, scanning for interesting patterns and textures in doors, streets, buildings, alleys and the blur of passing trains. But it was the deeper connection of portraits I really hoped to master.

Looking into people's eyes—whether through the lens or simply sitting on a busy street corner—I felt I could sense things like deep thought, prayer, happiness, inner peace, frustration. Without judgment or assumption, I'd try to link the moment to my own personal awareness. *Did this reality for millions of people—a bedlam of poverty juxtaposed with a tenacious vitality—shake them as much as it shook me?*

It was a difficult dichotomy to absorb. The vibrancy of the country struck me with awe: women in brightly coloured saris dusted with rose perfume; zephyrs of cardamom, black pepper and fennel wafting from the market; men shuttling rickshaws through busy streets; kids running happily to school with favourite books in hand; and the many devotees of diverse religions—always celebrating something.

And yet around the edges of this beauty swirled the kind of suffering that made you feel helpless—a woman in tattered rags with her dirt-covered children begging for food, an old man dying alone in a train station. I wanted to take all the pain away and love everyone. My heart was open to it all, but I couldn't have an emotional reaction anymore—I was just another visitor passing through.

I was trying to express myself in an unspoken language of truth and gratitude, but I simply didn't have the words to describe what I was experiencing any longer.

AIRPORTS

I came to see airports two ways: as places where many cultures merged into a single manic flow, and as benchmarks where I could meter my own changes as the world around me shifted.

Airports delivered a sensory overload you couldn't ignore. A structural jumble. A muddle of smells: sweat and jet fuel seeping through the walls, floral bouquets in damp tropic air. Audio mashups of wailing babies, squeaking luggage wheels, distorted public announcement systems that were incomprehensible even if you understood the language.

There were the glances shared with fellow travellers—faces filled with loss, confusion, grief, love, excitement and expectation, the waypoints of life. Where were they going? What were they leaving? And why?

Vignettes from outside the building… smoke lingering in inexplicable heat… icy blasts raking the tarmac… vans and taxis… a swirl of heads hurrying through a bricolage of unfamiliar technological clutter.

And me—the bewildered explorer, each destination a new transition to decipher. Did I waste too much time in these polished corridors? Time stirred with the guilt of contributing to the waste and pollution spewing into the world. My own inner disorder, I now believe, demanded I find solace in the kind of externalized chaos airports provided. Like the couloir in La Grave, they were a tool to test my balance—could I keep it together, stay focused and organized, manage money and not lose my passport?

When the shit hit the fan, as it inevitably did, airports also became arenas in which to practise patience—keeping calm during run-ins with border and military personnel, or staying composed in the face of graft-hungry police, damaged surfboards and $1,500 baggage fees.

Yet airports were also a space for introspection. Opportunities to walk with the mind, to question, to grow and learn to accept unwanted truths: the bags *are* missing, the flight *is* delayed, we have the *wrong* visas. They were places of true vulnerability when I was stuck or in pain and unable to communicate in the local language, but also welcome think tanks for considering how I might better pursue career aspirations, manage affairs of the heart, let go of something or hold on tighter.

Perhaps most important, airports were where you learned to truly appreciate the concept of "home"—waypoints that registered your gratitude in returning alive from a dangerous adventure, hopefully bearing the gifts of more poise, insight and wisdom.

Photo by Paul Morrison.

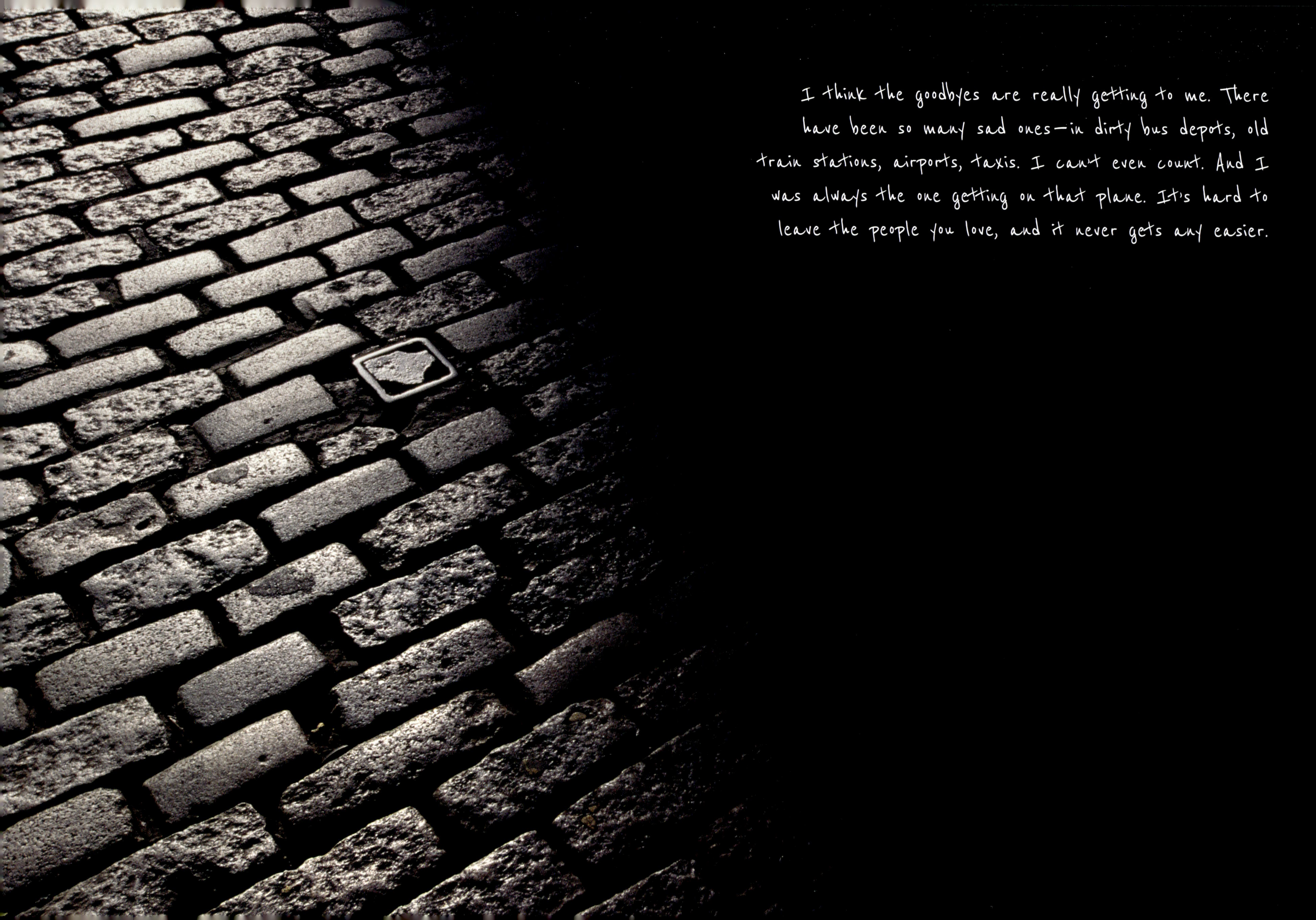

I think the goodbyes are really getting to me. There have been so many sad ones—in dirty bus depots, old train stations, airports, taxis. I can't even count. And I was always the one getting on that plane. It's hard to leave the people you love, and it never gets any easier.

Central train station, New Delhi, India.

Driving 3,500 kilometres through Iran's diversity of landscapes, our group was fascinated by the number of world heritage sites, elaborate city squares and decorative mosques that immediately connected us to the country's history. Eventually, dusty desert roads led us into the far reaches of soaring, snow-covered mountains where we found ourselves spellbound not by just the beauty of the land, but the quirks of local ski culture.

Alborz Mountains outside Tehran, Iran.

Ancient ruins of the Persepolis complex near Shiraz, Iran.

EL SALVADOR

One spring in Roatán, a beautiful, dark-eyed German girl appeared under the palm I was resting beneath and introduced herself. We were immediately attracted, but what I thought would be just another transient love affair evolved into a five-year relationship that required travelling more than a full day to visit her.

To reach her home in El Salvador, a ferry from Roatán would drop me at the Honduran port town of La Ceiba, where I'd catch a bus to San Pedro Sula and spend the night falling asleep to the sound of gunfire. At first light, I'd jump on a 15-hour "chicken bus" (a route on which passengers also transport produce and livestock) for the final bone-jarring haul over jungle-covered mountains to the Salvadoran capital, San Salvador. The potholed road was peppered with wandering animals, discarded vehicle parts and the odd "checkpoint" manned by thugs looking to loot the bus. But the trial was always worth it.

Travelling shaped our love—an invitation to the unknown that allowed us to indulge our mutual curiosity for the world. We spent some of the wildest times of our lives exploring Central America together, witnessing the charm and grace that abounded in village life as well as its flip side: horrific car accidents, people starving or wounded in gang-related violence. Often, we'd wake to the entire room shaking, car alarms pulsing and distressed neighbours running into the street as yet another earthquake hit this seismically active area.

Threading it all was the lightness of surfing. We spent much of our time checking out classic breaks around El Salvador, where the waves were often perfect. Shacking up in hostels, I'd often surf alone while she enjoyed beach life. Well-known spots like El Zonte, El Sunzal, La Libertad and Punta Mango saw few foreign surfers back then, and still had a natural, raw feeling. The beaches, however, could also be dangerous—in or out of the water. One time we were robbed of everything, left only with a reminder that no one could be trusted. Though Salvadorans on the whole were friendly and welcoming, abject poverty and gangs ruled these areas. We understood that these waves were all some local surfers had to live for, and tried to respect their space.

We spent some of the wildest times of our lives exploring Central America together, witnessing the charm and grace that abounded in village life as well as its flip side—horrific accidents, crushing poverty and frightening earthquakes.

Travelling circus, La Libertad, El Salvador.

CHECK ENG

PASCUA

Wandering the rugged coastline of Chile's remote Isla de Pascua, my only point of reference the crash of waves that had crossed an eternity of ocean to strike this iron shore, I stumbled across a fire glowing beneath the sagging darkness of an incoming storm. Sunburned and worn from circumnavigating the island over the past week, I sat down to warm my feet and reflect.

After journeying to the Canadian Arctic on a month-long ski expedition, I spent two months decompressing in Kauai and Indonesia, then made a brief stop in Whistler in preparation for a 4,000-kilometre road trip through Chile and Argentina for *A Skier's Journey*. After filming wrapped up, I flew to Pascua (a.k.a. Easter Island) to surf, dive and photograph the island's famous *moai*—mysterious giant statues that had enchanted me since childhood.

Though it was a bucket-list destination that should have invigorated me, too many back-to-back trips had combined to overwhelm me. I knew I was leading a privileged life, and was often still filled with joy—so why did I feel so beaten down? I looked to the heavens for answers.

I sat by the fire for hours, watching the coals crumble into ashes and reaching out to God. As my introspection deepened, the gunmetal sky briefly cracked to reveal shafts of light which, whimsically, I accepted as mute validation I was on the right path.

Rejuvenated, the following day found me anchored half a kilometre offshore under cumulus puffballs with my new friend Christian, a local free diver and spearfishing champion, decking ourselves out in spearfishing essentials: wetsuits, flippers, weight belt and bamboo spear guns. Jumping into the cold Pacific, we watched the boat disappear behind serious chop.

Demonstrating his technique, Christian dove 20 metres with ease in the crystal-clear water and surfaced with a fish on his spear. After repeating this several times in a row, it was my turn. I tilted my mask down to gaze at the round, car-sized boulders whizzing with colourful sea life, took a final breath and ducked under.

The fish were so deep it took a huge lungful of air not only to make it down, but for the patience required to take a shot. I badly wanted to spear a fish, and came close several times, but earnest commitment was no match for skill. After two hours, the cold infiltrated my wetsuit, my muscles grew weak and I accepted defeat.

Bringing my attention back above the surface, I was greeted by a shock. Christian and the boat were nowhere to be seen and the coast much farther away than where we'd jumped in. I was drifting out. Kicking hard to see above the rough seas, I swam towards shore. Stymied by a strong current, however, exhaustion and panic soon set in. Just as I was about to drop my weight-belt, Christian's hands appeared, waving between dark, rolling peaks. Back in the boat, my fear dissipated as we celebrated the dozen brightly hued fish that lay at his feet.

That night we feasted on fish and drank wine beneath a stunning firmament. Thanking Christian for sharing his ocean wisdom, I stumbled down the dusty road to my tent, grateful —once again, and not for the last time—to be alive.

A few of the journals accumulated after 20 years of travel. Photo by Jordan Manley.

Atlas Mountains, Morocco.

The several ranges of the Atlas Mountains arc between the Mediterranean and Atlantic coasts of North Africa. After successfully climbing and skiing their highest peak, 4,167-metre Mt. Toubkal, we made a ten-hour drive into the Sahara Desert to try our hand at skiing on gigantic sand dunes. Riding camels into a sea of golden waves, we set up camp as our guides prepared pizza over a fire on a traditional hot stone. Sipping wine under a full moon that illuminated the desert, we listened to stories of those who'd crossed this forbidding land using only stars as a guide.

Today I called a friend from a payphone like I used to do from random airports and far-off countries, feeling it's important to stay connected to certain people while away on an adventure. I'm a bit unsure as to what might happen on this trip, so I felt comfort in expressing my fears in the moment to him. But hanging up, I wondered if it might be the last time he heard my voice.

Photo by Daniel Ronnback.

COSTA RICA

The enticement of a new destination had me hanging out the bus window, taking in what I could in the darkness as we bounced down a steep dirt road into the Costa Rican beach town of Santa Teresa. When the bus drove away, I waited for the dust to settle into the night, holding only my surfboard and a small backpack, unsure where to go. After reading about this beautiful surfer's idyll, it felt surreal to have arrived.

On that first occasion of many, I immediately sensed an intense energy. Like the mountain towns I was accustomed to, Santa Teresa magnetized travellers of every ethnicity and culture, attracting people who had no filter on self-expression—authentic, uncensored, wild souls. There were parties, lust and romance, a vortex stirred by amazing waves, dense jungle and a lack of societal rules. I could relate to the disarray.

After 20-plus visits to "Santa T," the memories of days spent at a rustic beach house are still some of my most precious. Sitting on the porch as rain danced on the tin roof, the worries of the greater world were stilled by conversations about surfing, travel and broken hearts, the silences between words charged by crashing waves and thunderstorms that lit up the sky.

Among the many friendships I made there were people who actively helped with my healing—physiotherapists, massage therapists, reiki masters. One in particular stripped me to the bone during a memorable rainy season; three days a week for the better part of three months, he dug into the traumas held fast in my tissues until I cried for mercy.

The more time I spent there, the more I fell in love with it—and with the ocean. Sitting on my board in the line-up washed in morning light, I admired pelicans gliding just above the lip of perfect A-frame peaks. The waves were also a training ground: I learned to read the water, navigate heavy beach breaks and charge low-tide tubes. Though a humbling, beautiful, often spiritual experience, the very best of me shone through in Santa T.

Wall mural by David Michael Perry, Zeneidas Surf Garden, Costa Rica.

paz
2012
one love
JAH

Photo by Paul Morrison.

Without faith in something, I would
be empty and alone in this world.

Photo by Jason Thompson.

Shadows in the Snow

SECTION VIII

LEFT Photo by Jordan Manley. RIGHT Photo by Ben Thouard.

SHADOWS

Sitting on my board at sunset in a dozen tropical seas, the water dappled in a thousand colours, I entertained a recurring thought: although every place I'd sought refuge had brought me a deeper sense of time and space, and each new experience something to learn and grow from, the act of surfing—the weightlessness, the gliding, the commitment and the communing with powerful natural forces—somehow always turned my eyes back to the mountains, which dwelt like shadows in my soul. Incrementally and unexpectedly, these realizations made stepping back into my skis seem not only possible, but desirable.

Photo by Jason Thompson.

REBOOT

Over the years, a spring ski-mountaineering mission became something of a tradition. When Forrest Cootes invited me on an expedition with a couple of American acquaintances to ski 5,193-metre Mt. Shkhara, highest point in Georgia's Caucasus Mountains, I said yes to my first big trip alongside a crew I wasn't wholly familiar with.

Most of the 15-hour drive from the capital of Tbilisi to the staging village of Ushguli was serene: green, rolling hills streaked with pink cherry blossoms; lush valleys lined with crystal-clear creeks; birds flocking across moody skies. Nearing our destination, however, peaceful turned stressful as our drunken driver piloted the van up a steep road that narrowed to a single lane, high above a canyon—where we found ourselves negotiating for hours with police before being granted access.

In stormy Ushguli, our four-person crew hunkered down with a family, enjoying *khachapuri* (cheese-stuffed bread) and *kharcho* (barley soup). When the weather cleared we set out on the first leg, feeling vulnerable as we skinned across a basin between massive, snow-loaded slopes. Settling into our acclimatization camp, the surrounding terrain appeared perfect: broad moraines offering safe approaches, steep powder lines of variable consequence and some technical ice that begged climbing. After 10 days exploring the area we hauled our gear to a final base camp, grinding nine hours through a whiteout. Snow conditions felt good, the crew was strong and we agreed to go for it the following day.

Warm and safe in my sleeping bag, I tried to calm myself with positivity, but all I could conjure were the risks of climbing a steep, icy, 1,800-metre face. Departing in the wee hours, we navigated crevasses in the darkness, tracking each other by the sounds of breathing and rasping skis, reaching the base of the wall at sunrise.

As we climbed, pink and blue brushed the peaks behind us, a softness that contrasted the extreme exposure we were courting and the danger posed by a massive icefall above. After speeding up the first 1,200 metres of the face, we reached the base of the couloir and made the call to press on. The sprint wouldn't last; only 250 metres below the summit, the leader found blue ice lurking beneath the snow. Our climb was over.

Plugging an ice-screw into the slope, he tied himself in and threw the rope down for the rest of us to do the same. Awash in defeat, cognizant that the entire face could rip out at any moment, the sun suddenly peeked over the summit, bathing us in warmth, as though Shkhara was honouring our decision to retreat.

Conditions were too dangerous to ski safely until the snow softened. In a blur of disappointment and fatigue, we built a small ledge and waited four hours for the surface to thaw. At one point, I dozed off and stopped myself from falling at the last second. It was the signal to go. We skied cautiously in calculated sections, ensuring no one's slough hit the skier below them. Eventually, we arrived back in camp all smiles, secure in the knowledge that despite the time, money and expectation poured into an expedition, it was the courage and experience to know when *not* to push it that was the greatest achievement of all.

LEFT Ushguli, Caucasus Mountains, Georgia. Photo by Jason Thompson. **RIGHT** Photo by Jason Thompson.

Mount Shkhara, Georgian Caucasus. Photo by Jason Thompson.

When you're climbing steep, icy slopes, every step and tool placement is an act of commitment, focus and faith.
You can do everything right, but I knew all too well that in a split second the mountains could discard you.

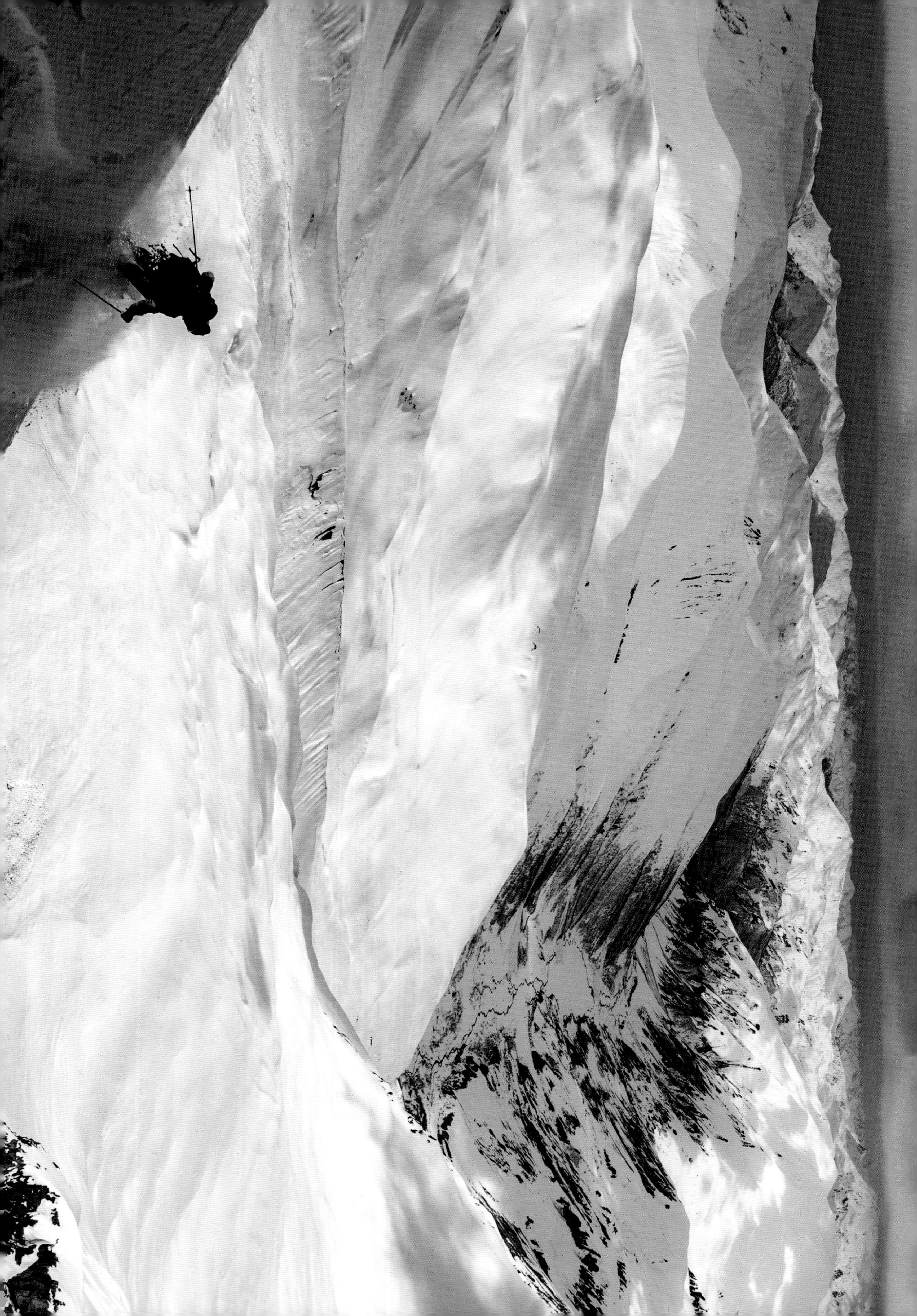

LEFT Finishing a run on the lower flank of Mount Shkhara, Georgian Caucasus. Photo by Jason Thompson. **RIGHT** Georgian hosts. Photo by Jason Thompson.

The imposing Bec des Rosses, Verbier, Switzerland. Photo by David Carlier.

VERBIER

If there was a single peak I longed to reckon with it was the Bec des Rosses, overlooking Verbier ski area in Switzerland's Pennine Alps. Here, on a steep north-facing slope with exposure at every turn, the Verbier Xtreme, the world's most prestigious freeskiing event, took place every April. As a competitive athlete, this ultimate test had always been a goal, and after eight years away from the professional circuit I found my mind circling back.

Tracking down the event's director, I shared my backstory of successful competition, sidelining injuries and desire to add this missing career milestone. I begged for a wildcard berth; he said he'd consider it and to check back in at registration in a few weeks.

Despite having drifted far from the competitive milieu, I still pined for its challenge and intensity—the energy of the crowd, the hunger of skiers ready to give it their all, the anticipation as the line of contestants grew ever shorter until you stood in the gate and the starter called: *three… two… one!* Then the rush of being the only skier on an entire mountain, charging fast and fluidly, an inner voice saying *Breathe—you can do this!*

It felt like personal unfinished business; I'd promised myself a return to the competitive world as soon as I was again skiing on two feet. Healthier than I had been in years, there was only lingering mild discomfort; all the surfing, physiotherapy and self-healing had paid off. It felt liberating to ski outside of survival mode, truly appreciating the beauty and freedom of mountains again. The further the pain had subsided, the more a welcome shadow in the snow—the once fearless young man with a burning desire to never give up—had revealed himself in me.

But my wildcard wasn't to be. Weather concerns had already made it questionable whether even the seeded athletes would get their runs in, making it too much of a gamble to add an outside competitor. I was offered a forerunning position—the chance to test the course before the competitors skied it. But knowing I would have skied it as hard as in any contest regardless of consequences, it seemed all risk and no reward; I turned it down.

Though part of me was disappointed, another felt immense relief. And in that realization dwelt another lesson: it was time to let go of something that, in reality, perished long ago.

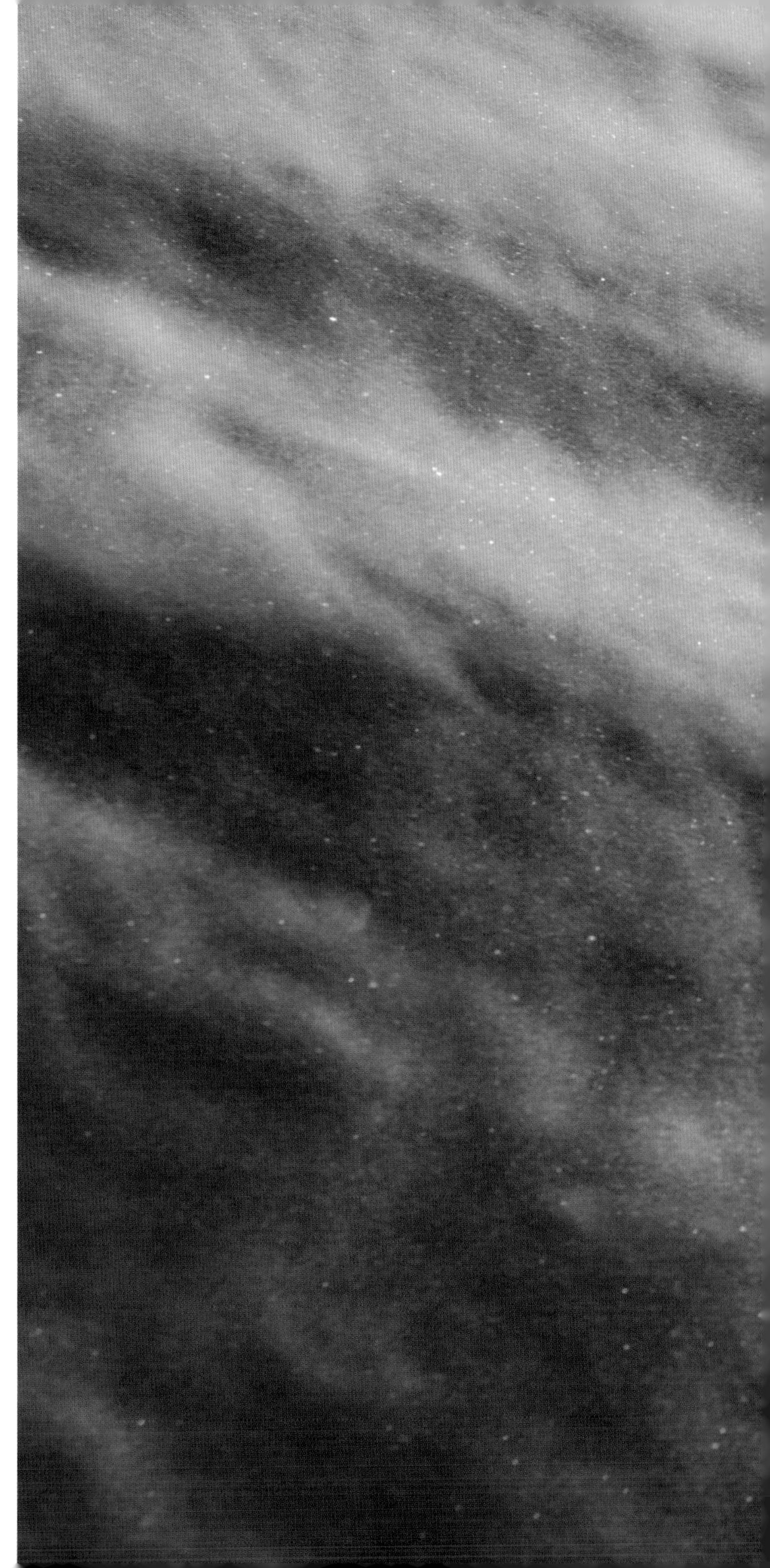

LEFT Photo by Daniel Ronnback. **RIGHT** Photo by Mattias Fredriksson.

Returning to competition feels like personal unfinished business. The further my physical pain has subsided, the more the once fearless young man with a burning desire to never give up has revealed himself to me.

LEFT Saint Cristophe en Oisans, near La Grave, France. Photo by Jordan Manley. **RIGHT** Photo by Oskar Enander.

MENTOR

I met Steve Ogle in Southern Chile in 2000. Late one evening he stumbled into a hostel where I was staying, soaked and Argus-eyed, and an instant bond was formed. We would end up travelling the globe together—skiing, climbing and generally having epic adventures in otherworldly places.

Like myself, Steve was born and raised in Ontario but now lives in British Columbia. A biologist by training and photographer by vocation, he's witty and educated with an outlook based on empirical fact. A hockey lover who can skate like the wind, he's passing on his ice skills as a dedicated father to two rambunctious boys. Though we shared a passion for exploration, it was his ability to push into uncharted landscapes with both confidence and caution that opened me up to his experience and knowledge. Trusting Steve's intuition when things got real in the mountains had saved our skin more than once, and it was largely from him that I learned the value of true partnership.

We also shared a mutual love for Patagonia, where we made our first big trip together. In 2004 we'd spent 30 days—most of them stormbound in a tent—on the Southern Patagonian Ice Field, running out of food and barely making it out alive. But the powerful landscapes and wild weather left an indelible impression, and we returned several times. Combining ski expeditions with photo road trips and other exploratory objectives, we spent weeks on Patagonia's dusty open roads with no real destination in mind, staying alert on the heavily caffeinated local tea known as *maté*. Spontaneous suggestions such as driving 1,000 kilometres to Buenos Aires simply to have "the best steak of our lives" weren't uncommon.

On expeditions from the jungles of Colombia to the summit of Mt. Logan, not only have we seen much together but also pushed each other physically—often mercilessly. Over the years, I've learned from Steve what it's like to be bold and courageous in everything from managing risk in the mountains to gaining balance in life.

Steve Ogle fords a stream during the Darwin Traverse. Tierra del Fuego, Chile. Photo by Kari Medig.

LEFT Torres Del Paine National Park, Chilean Patagonia. Photo by Steve Ogle. **RIGHT** Ptor Spricenieks, Chad Sayers and Steve Ogle on the summit of Pico Simón Bolívar, Colombia. Photo by Steve Ogle.

Photo by Steve Ogle.

LOGAN

My introduction to Mt. Logan, Canada's highest peak at 5,957 metres, was a piece in *Alpinist* magazine recounting stories of those willing to suffer unremitting pain—even death—to stand atop it. The supreme climbing challenge that Logan presented drew me in.

In May 2017 our five-man team landed by ski plane on the Quintino Sella Glacier at the toe of King's Trench, the most popular and least-technical route up the mountain. The next 17 days would be a willing sufferfest, gaining 3,500 metres of vertical over 23 kilometres to reach the summit plateau. I had done longer trips, but the combination of altitude, extreme weather and remoteness made Logan one of the most gruelling.

For a week we moved slowly and steadily up a system of glaciers, pulling heavily laden sleds through two major storms. When the terrain steepened at King's Col, we stashed the sleds and began shuttling loads to ever-higher camps. As elevation increased, so did the psychological battle to drive the body forward, heart pounding like a drum and lungs gasping for air: one day you'd take the lead on the rope, dragging your partner up the mountain, and the next day he'd be dragging you. Skirting crevasses hundreds of metres deep, we worked our way through house-sized seracs and apartment-sized blocks of blue ice. The unfathomable scale revealed the pale insignificance of our humanity.

As did the cold. Averaging –30°C without wind chill, setting up camp after 15-hour days was doubly hard and came with the ever-present spectre of losing your feet. As a reminder, each morning saw us wake to a thick blanket of frost on our sleeping bags.

On Day 13, we erected our fourth and final camp on Logan's vast summit plateau. With a circumference of 30 kilometres and 11 peaks over 5,000 metres, should weather move in—a common occurrence—finding your way back up and over the entrance col at 5,300 metres was near impossible and often fatal.

Setting out for the summit next morning, we were eight hours in with 200 vertical metres to go when the wind picked up and the cold really sank in. We dug a hole in a snowdrift to shelter and regroup. With limited food and energy remaining and a forecast of worsening weather, two opted to throw in the towel while the rest of us made a final push. Dropping everything we carried, we headed out with only ice axes in hand. Punch-drunk in a fog on the dizzying summit ridge, we pressed on, driven by the knowledge that stopping meant freezing to death. An hour later we broke into sunshine and celebrated on the pyramidal summit.

On the descent back to camp we met the other two heading up. They'd decided to go for it after all and would soon summit themselves, making the entire experience a group success—affirmation of how you could be beaten down day after day in the mountains but in the end find the inner strength to achieve more than what you thought possible.

LEFT Ferrying loads up the King's Trench on Mt. Logan, B.C. Photo by Steve Ogle. **RIGHT** Photo by Jordan Manley.

There's this voice inside that tells you to keep going, and when you listen, it can fuel your motivation and hardness. It's what gets you to the top.

LEFT Photo by Steve Ogle. **RIGHT** Skiing down after summiting Mt. Logan, King's Peak in the background. Photo by Steve Ogle.

Photo by Jason Thompson.

PRECIOUS

In September 2018, I returned to Nepal and the Himalaya, the range that had inspired 20 years of travel. As on that first trip, excitement and nervousness followed as I exited the Kathmandu airport into the wee hours of the night. Instead of a wide-eyed neophyte with a loose agenda, however, this time three friends and I planned to climb and ski an unconquered 7,000-metre peak in the country's remote northwest: Mt. Saipal.

In the new millennium, the area had seen little attention from the Western world due to a Maoist insurgence and difficult travel logistics. Sixteen days later—most of them spent weaving along exposed mountain roads in a packed jeep before undertaking a week-long trek through Nepal's wild west—we set up base camp in a stunning alpine meadow at 3,500 metres. We eventually set high camp inside an icy bergschrund at 5,700 metres below the final pitch, a 1,500-metre face that led to a razor-thin ridge and the hidden summit.

After three weeks of acclimatization we set out from high camp for a first attempt at the peak, having ditched our skis after discovering the mountain wasn't skiable. I was feeling physically strong and mentally comfortable with the exposure, but two-thirds of the way up, at 6,400 metres, cold was again my demise. Frostbite set into both feet and continuing farther would have meant risking their loss.

Spent and cold, we descended to basecamp to reset. The night before our second attempt one of the team became ill, and the pair who decided to go for it anyway had their tent half-buried by sloughing snow in the bergschrund high camp and solemnly retreated. We accepted defeat.

On the walk back to the village of Talkot, I came across a cell phone on the trail playing music. Thinking someone ahead had likely dropped it, I passed it to the head Sherpa. Around midnight, I awoke to an angry mob outside my tent. A porter hadn't returned to camp and, as the phone belonged to him, I was somehow now responsible for his whereabouts.

Heading back up the narrow path in the dark to search, I was pierced by the burning glares of thirty men who periodically shoved and accused me of murder. After five tense hours of this, the situation escalated. But just as it felt a fight to the death was inevitable, a handful of mountain police appeared like angels in the night to enforce a peaceful solution.

The porter's body was eventually located, far below the track. A single misstep had sent the young man tumbling 500 metres. We watched as the corpse, wrapped in a red sheet, was hauled up and carried back to Talkot where his family and friends mourned while we awaited the jeeps. It was utter sadness.

The mountain had turned us back, but like any expedition we came away with another affirmation of the preciousness—and precariousness—of life.

LEFT Climbing above 6,000 metres on Mt. Saipal, Nepal. Photo by Jason Thompson. **RIGHT** Photo by Jason Thompson.

ABOVE Photos by Jason Thompson, upper left by Chad Sayers. **RIGHT** Photo by Jason Thompson.

Mountains offer you the chance to respect something that
is so much greater than yourself or the material world.

HEART

Dressed in white, a Kogi priest known as a *Mamo* chanted a mixture of Spanish and his own dialect while masticating a wad of coca leaf. Tying a string around each of our wrists, he offered a blessing for the journey on which he'd now guide us.

Steve Ogle, ski-mountaineer Ptor Spricenieks and I had been granted rare permission to enter the Sierra Nevada de Santa Marta in Colombia. Back in 1999, Ptor had tried accessing the range from both sides but was denied, its Indigenous gatekeepers leery of foreigners entering the sacred mountains they called the "Heart of the World." Only a couple weeks out from the lynch-mob incident in the western Himalaya, I was on edge myself, fearful of trusting the Kogi.

With donkeys hauling our gear and four eager young porters—one clad only in gumboots, a t-shirt and ragged pants—we followed the Mamo into dense jungle. Our objective, some 60 kilometres distant, was to climb and ski Pico Simón Bolívar, Colombia's second highest mountain at 5,730 metres.

Like bugs fighting their way out of a spider's web, we started by clawing our way through a tangle of plants that tugged at every protuberance—limbs, heads, the skis on our back. Before we could enjoy any sense of accomplishment, things began to quickly unravel. As the terrain steepened on Day 2, it was clear we'd have to ditch the donkeys. With the porters already overloaded, we were forced to leave half our food and gear behind. Worse, the Mamo—the only one of us who knew the actual route—became ill and retreated.

Pressing on, we had only the young porters and their intuitive connection with the land to rely on. Though courageous in their desire to help us navigate through soaring passes and yawning valleys, it took but a single day before we found ourselves lost, hungry and dehydrated. Forced to relinquish the ground we'd gained to find water and rest, we retreated in the dark, downclimbing an exposed face shrouded in mist. Feeling feeble on the descent, I experienced an out-of-body state, haunted by the vision of a porter slipping and disappearing into the void, as had happened in Nepal.

Day after day, dawn to dark, we pushed up dangerously steep slopes, unsure we would make it. As elevation increased and vegetation thinned, the muddy trail transitioned to ledges of golden grass that meandered past emerald lakes into scrub alpine and expanses of exposed granite. Condors soaring over a sea of peaks—and the unsettling sight of stumbling across a plane wreck—distracted us from our exhaustion and any thought of the outside world. On Day 12 we finally reached high base camp.

Although the route was now straightforward, the summit was distant enough that we started at 3 a.m. Touching snow after such a long approach may have felt slightly foreign, but the bite of crampons on ice also lifted our spirits. Compared to the previous weeks' struggle, the 14-hour trek was physically undemanding. Yet because we'd so often thought we wouldn't make it, standing atop the peak was special enough to make the pleasure of gliding down the mountain on skis feel almost anticlimactic.

To make it home safely we'd have to retrace our hard-won steps with barely enough food to survive, but reaching the Heart of the World made our own hearts lighter than air.

LEFT A Kogi Mamo shares his coca leaves in the Sierra Nevada de Santa Marta, Colombia. Photo by Steve Ogle.

LEFT Approaching the final section of Pico Simón Bolívar in the Sierra Nevada de Santa Marta, Colombia. Photo by Steve Ogle. **CENTRE + RIGHT** Photos by Steve Ogle.

It's here, in the hands of Mother Nature and the elements that we're tested—an opportunity to discover a true self that dwells just on the other side of fear. For me, that's what gives this journey meaning.

LEFT • RIGHT Photos by Steve Ogle.

Photo by Eric Berger

HOME

After travelling the world in pursuit of the ultimate ski expedition, it was perhaps ironic that we'd find it close to home on the west coast of British Columbia. Our team of three was attempting to walk, ski and float our way up and over the icy spine of the Coast Mountains to the Pacific Ocean for a long-delayed and final episode of *A Skier's Journey.*

The night before departure we congregated around a fire at the edge of Chilko Lake, its windless tranquility belying an arduous journey that would see us loaded down with skis, packrafts and enough food to reach our first of three caches. In the morning, a man of about 60 who'd fled busy Germany for a more peaceful life in the wilds of B.C. boated us across the lake to the pebbled shores of Franklin Arm. I'm sure he saw part of himself in our younger, adventurous spirits.

Over 13 long kilometres we forged our own trail through the wilderness: navigating deadfall and dense forest, wading cold rivers, staying sharp for signs of grizzly bears. Each footstep was a mindful one—an injury out here would make for a near-impossible rescue.

After five days we began a 65-kilometre crossing of the Homathko Icefield. Bagging a half-dozen peaks over 21 days through some of the most beautiful landscapes I'd ever seen, we finally reached our last and largest objective: Mount Grenville. Conditions were perfect as we began the climb: cold snow, unaffected by wind. A few hours of climbing got us to the summit just in time to lose the sun behind a cloud; we waited, ready to drop in at a moment's notice. An hour later, the cameraman, stationed below, radioed about a potential window of light. The envelope of white slowly lifted as red sunlight illuminated the line below. Dropping in, I skied a twisting whaleback spine into an icy chute. Turning between the walls, I rallied my way towards the line's final obstacle—a mandatory jump across a large bergschrund. But as I was about to make the leap, the sun once again slipped behind a cloud. With zero depth perception, I hit the rock-solid ice on the bergschrund's far side, smashing my knee into my face and cartwheeling 100 metres to a bloody halt.

Lying motionless, breathing deeply, I tried to gauge the pain in my knee as blood poured from my mouth. I didn't want to panic, but I was clearly injured and we were five days from pickup. Though my ski partner helped me down to the flats, standing on the knee was difficult. I skinned slowly back to camp and began icing while the crew packed up. I now had two options: call in a rescue or suffer through the remainder. Knowing that pulling out would severely impact the storyline of the series, I chose the latter.

Ahead were three more days of travelling complex glaciated terrain pulling fully loaded sleds, then a 2,500-vertical-metre bushwhack descent to a river that would then require two days of packrafting to reach Bute Inlet on the Pacific. But with the help and support of my teammates and a well-honed pain tolerance, we were ultimately able to finish.

In what seemed an almost comic echo of much of my ski career, it took everything I had to persevere, but in the end, crossing home through the wildness of British Columbia had been the most breathtaking and satisfying journey of all.

LEFT Camp on the Homathko Icefield, B.C. Photo by Jordan Manley. **RIGHT** Photo by Jordan Manley.

Nothing lasts,
nothing is finished...
nothing is perfect.

LEFT Photo by Jordan Manley. **RIGHT** A fog briefly lifts during a traverse of the Homathko Icefield, B.C. Photo by Jordan Manley.

LEFT Snowfall Lodge, Selkirk Mountains, B.C. Photo by Steve Ogle. **RIGHT** Tantalus Range, Squamish, B.C. Photo by Guy Fattal.

LEFT Photo by Mattias Fredriksson. **RIGHT** Photo by Guy Fattal. **FOLLOWING SPREAD** Photo by Jordan Manley.

Chad Sayers and daughter Aiya at home in Whistler, B.C. Photo by Paul Morrison.

Epilogue

I remember sitting on airplanes, oceans passing beneath the wings, trying to start this story time and time again. But I really had no idea where to begin.

There seemed much to say, but I didn't have the words—or a direction. Was it the solitude and grandeur found in wild places that I wanted to share? Or the commitment and silent hardships of an athlete that now yearned for an outlet? Perhaps it was the spirituality I believed kept me safe all these years that I needed to celebrate. I didn't know. I was confused and uncertain about where the story lay—or if there was one at all.

Eventually, a few savvy friends helped me understand that the very uncertainty I had long embraced *was* the story. You'll find their names up front, and I'm forever indebted to the vision, patience and professionalism they brought to organizing and curating this project. The names of several other friends adorn their amazing photos—images that tell a story I could never hope to articulate. And there are many others to thank in this journey, from a wonderful family who always had my back, to the ski partners, sponsors, healers and friends made along the way. You know who you are, and I salute you.

Assembling this book has been its own tale of halting uncertainty. An eight-year odyssey that began with nebulous questions but ultimately delivered a definitive answer: while skiing, climbing and surfing have brought me expression, humility and reflection in equal measure, travel, more than anything, has been my teacher, sparking a passion to share the lessons held in its experiences. I'm now very clear about the simple reason behind this book: a vessel to inspire others to travel and explore in the way I was once inspired, to find their own beauty and truths amidst the challenges.

Of course, we must all evolve, moving beyond the familiar routines (and uncertainties) that define us. And life doesn't wait for you to get used to those changes. My world completely shifted with the arrival of a baby girl. Like many first-time parents, part of me was overjoyed at the thought, another part terrified that my freewheeling lifestyle would contract. But I soon learned—again like other parents—that a child expands your life, teaching you to love unconditionally and surrender to something more profound than your own existence. And so, this record also stands as a gift to little Aiya, who will doubtless find her own path to certainty.